Murder in The Lehigh Valley

D1557157

by
Katherine Ramsland
In Collaboration with
Zachary Lysek

Second Chance Publications
Gettysburg, PA 17325

TABLE OF CONTENTS

ACKNOWLEDGMENTS

It's not possible to write a book of this nature without assistance from people willing to pass along some tales, so we have several people to thank for making this collection possible. We'd like to acknowledge the following: Cathy Bitting, Natalie Boch, Dana DiVito, Colleen Lavdar, Susan Lysek, Nancy O'Hanlon, Joe Pochron, Joe Reichel, Al Stempo and Bucky Szulborski.

Special thanks also to Mark and Carol Nesbitt, who encouraged us to write this book and who shepherded the publication process.

PART I: DEATH AND THE VALLEY

The Valley

As idyllic as eastern Pennsylvania's Lehigh Valley may be, there's an unexpected dark side. Serial killers, mass murderers, violent gangs and outright hit men have all operated here, along with high-profile family killers. Even before these incidents, we had several Indian massacres and some homicides that made forensic history. In these pages we'll look at historical and contemporary murders, as well as some not yet solved.

In Pennsylvania during the mid-1700s, settlers leased the land where they resided, whereas in other states residents generally purchased land and owned the deed. Near Wilkes-Barre was a place called the Wyoming Valley, which settlers from both Pennsylvania and Connecticut sought to claim. There ensued several armed struggles as each side tried to force the other out. In 1765, the fertile area was declared part of Northampton County, but that didn't stop the Connecticut "Yankees" from trying yet again to grab it from the "Pennamites." At one point, the Yankees enlisted a group of lawless thugs and murderers known as the Paxton Boys to assist them, and they committed more illegal acts. The Northampton County sheriff formed a posse to arrest members of this gang, and on January 20, 1771, when Deputy Sheriff Nathan Ogden approached the outlaws, they shot and killed him. He thus became the first law enforcement officer in colonial Pennsylvania to lose his life in the line of duty.

The Lehigh Valley, covering Lehigh and Northampton Counties, was cultivated by several Native American tribes, notably the Lenni Lenape, who hunted and quarried jasper. Europeans came around 1700, and William Penn's sons acquired a wide swath of land during an infamous swindle known as the Walking Purchase. Indian raids took the lives of many white settlers, but the new residents soon forced the tribes to migrate west. A band of Moravians arrived in 1740 from Georgia, acquiring land in what we now know as Nazareth, and then settling central Bethlehem on the Lehigh River. By the end of that century, the region became a flourishing commercial settlement linked to outside businesses by a canal and railroad. The area grew prominent in the production of iron and steel. Directly after the Civil War, Asa Packer founded Lehigh University and in 1904 Bethlehem Steel became a dominating concern. By World War II, the area had encouraged silk manufacturing.

The Valley, framed by the Saucon Mountains, is a thriving place, but no human settlement is without tensions and attractions that can erupt in murder.

When Dana DeVito and I wrote a book called *Bethlehem Ghosts*, I became aware that this area had sustained quite a few unique homicidal incidents. Thus, I asked Zachary Lysek, the Northampton County Coroner, to team up with me to explore this violent terrain. While the Valley also encompasses Lehigh County, with Coroner Scott Grim and his deputies, I've come to know Zack well enough to talk with him at length about these cases.

Pennsylvania uses a coroner system and Zack Lysek has been coroner in Northampton County since 1992. Unlike most other counties in Pennsylvania, he's not elected to his position but appointed. He's been a police officer, a diener (assistant to a pathologist), a medical investigator, a security manager and a deputy coroner. As a death investigator, he has experience with homicide from several angles. To better understand what he does, let's look at how the American system of coroners evolved.

The Crowners

Prior to the *Magna Carta*, England's *Charts of Privileges* listed an office for the original death investigators in A.D. 925. Over two centuries later, in 1194, the judicial circuit in medieval England officially recorded in the *Articles of Eyre* that "crowners" were the *custodes placitorum coronæ*, or the keepers of the King's pleas. Those who held the office—soon to be called coroners—collected taxes, but also summoned inquest juries for suspicious fatal incidents. An inquest involved the gathering of seven to eleven "good men," who listened to evidence and circumstances and then voted on a verdict, although the coroner's opinion could influence the final decision.

Eventually the office, which remained political, evolved into that of a death investigator. By the 13th century coroners examined all dead bodies to determine the nature of wounds or diseases, as well as the manner of death. In the interest of community health or justice, they also summoned physicians to perform autopsies.

This system came to the U.S.—formerly the British colonies—and while a number of states have evolved into a medical examiner system, wherein the death investigator has at least a medical degree and often a specialty in pathology, most Pennsylvania counties have retained their coroners. A forensic pathologist does the autopsy, but the coroner or deputy coroner goes to a death scene to make decisions about the time, cause and manner of death. He or she could empanel a coroner's jury, although it's rare, and can order exhumations. The coroner relies on investigative skills, similar to a detective, including observation, awareness of the stages of death in diverse circumstances, and knowledge about whatever research must be done for an accurate analysis.

Northampton County Coroner's Office

Before Zack was appointed in Northampton, he served under coroner Joe Reichel, who'd held the position since 1962. Zack and I paid a call on Joe one afternoon at one of his funeral parlors to talk about the cases he remembered. A feisty man who dislikes monotony, he clearly enjoyed reminiscing. His first day on the job he had to deal with a bad call by an officer who had declared a woman the victim of a suicide. The problem was, she was shot square in the back of the head. Joe saw his share of gang murders, mostly drug and motorcycle gangs, and one that he recalled from the 1980s was like something out of Arthur Conan Doyle's *Hound of the Baskervilles*. They had to look for a body in the woods in Williams Township, an area engulfed in superstition. It was a cold November day and mist was rising from the ground. Difficult visibility only compounded the problem of figuring out just where this body had been buried, but then Joe saw something unusual: in the midst of all the wild growth was a tree that had a different appearance. It was from a nursery, so he said, "This is where the body is." And he was right.

Joe recounted a number of cases with which he had experience, from a vengeance seeking killer who set a fire that ended the lives of five children, to a woman who killed her husband by having her own daughter load and fire the .357 magnum. An attorney who staged a scene with an axe wanted to keep the axe, and a shooter using a home-made gun watched the weapon disintegrate after its first use—which was fatal. A victim of a bow-and-arrow assault had a target on his chest, while a body left near Martin's Creek bore marks from car tires.

Several of Joe's cases were unsolved and will show up in Part V of this book, but the first tales we'll recount date back much further than Joe's tenure.

Witch Attack

In *Bethlehem Ghosts*, Dana and I wrote about reported sightings of a spirit that arose from a historic murder in Easton. While the incident has not been affirmed as factual, it's an unusual tale of a collective fatal assault, so it belongs in this book as well. We'll just dispense with the supernatural part.

The story dates back to 1851, and is titled "The Fate of a Flirt of the Olden Times." A socially prominent American writer, Elizabeth F. Ellet, published it in *Godey's Lady's Book*, and it was reprinted in an historical account of the Valley. Many Easton residents—at least those who embrace history—are familiar with it.

This event apparently occurred when Easton was just a rural, wooded settlement. Residents tended to keep to themselves and were not keen about change of any kind, so the arrival of strangers got their attention. An Englishman, "Mr. Winton," purchased a house on North Fourth Street, in the building that now houses the *Express-Times*.

First, the furniture came and then a man, woman, and seven-year-old boy. Winton turned out to be a jovial, outspoken fellow, and a member of the Colonial Assembly. He'd brought his small family "to rusticate for a season" on the Delaware. They'd lived among the wealthy in cities like Paris and Philadelphia, so they were more sophisticated than the typical Easton family. That in itself was apparently threatening. Worse, Mrs. Winton was stunningly beautiful. She had long black hair and a perfect figure, and she wore flowing skirts that bespoke a lack of modesty. Not only that, she laughed too easily and had a flirty quality. "In short, she appeared to the untutored judgment of the dames of the village decidedly wanting in reserve."

It's no surprise, though, that the men enjoyed having her in their midst. They began offering their services when her husband was not around, inspiring jealousy from the other females—especially when Mrs. Winton failed to follow proper protocol for social engagements. Yet attempts by the women to ostracize her had little effect, as she had no trouble finding company from male admirers. When her husband left to attend to business in Philadelphia, the women noticed more male callers to Mrs. Winton's home, and the groundwork was laid for trouble.

As the story goes, that fall Mrs. Winton and her son went riding into a wooded area. When a bird spooked her horse, a man appeared to grab the reins and steady it. He was new to Mrs. Winton and she lost no time in charming him. He became a regular visitor. The neighbor women began to gossip endlessly about the men who were in and out of the house, passing rumors that this shameless coquette must be consorting with supernatural entities to make men bend so easily to her will. They were determined to reveal her for the witch she was, so they called a meeting one evening and when it was dark, they donned black masks and went looking for their prey.

They grabbed Mrs. Winton in her house, binding and gagging her, and in the presence of her pleading son, dragged her into the woods. In a pond, they dunked her over and over as punishment for stealing the attention of their husbands. They left her on the bank and returned to their own homes.

But Mrs. Winton did not survive the overbearing assault. Her body was found the next day by the pond. Although an investigation got under way, the perpetrators kept a conspiratorial silence, so no one was ever arrested for this murder. Popular opinion, at least among the women, seemed to hold that the victim had been justly punished for engaging in witchcraft and her death was just an unfortunate side-effect.

Original Location of the Pond

Early Forensics

In the Delaware River, just off Easton's bank, is Getters Island, with an upstream tip that nearly touches Pennsylvania's bank. The small strip of land was named for Charles Goetter, or Götter, now often spelled Getter. A German immigrant, he was courting two women in 1833, Molly Hummer and Margaret Lawall, although he was in love only with Molly. When Margaret claimed she was pregnant, perhaps to force him to decide between them, Charles reluctantly married her, but refused to live with her as man and wife. He'd apparently once said, "I'll have Molly Hummer if I have to walk on pins to get her."

Margaret worked as a maid on the estate of Peter Wagener and shortly after the wedding, when she was heavy with child, Charles came one night to take her for a walk. The next morning, her corpse was found in a quarry by Greenwood Avenue. Getter, the prime suspect, was arrested, but he refused to confess, so preparations commenced for a trial. Getter engaged the services of a famous and skillful lawyer, James Madison Porter, who helped found Lafayette College. This alone made the proceedings sensational. With no witnesses to the incident, it appeared to be an easy case for this masterful attorney to win, but he had not counted on a young doctor who lived in the area and who had avidly studied the emerging forensic sciences.

During the 19th century, some American physicians had noticed that participating in a criminal case that garnered public interest could generate fame and advancement, just as celebrity trials do even today. In addition, these cases had proven a productive venue for demonstrating what the new medical science could do. Up to this point, only medicine and toxicology had made a forensic impact, and doctors in America looked to noted figures in France who had founded medico-legal programs in several prestigious universities. Dr. Samuel Gross, 28, had taken a course in medical jurisprudence at the Jefferson Medical School in Philadelphia. Unable to develop a practice there, he'd returned to his hometown, Easton. He thus ended up as a witness for the prosecution in the Getter case.

The trial commenced on August 19, 1833, lasting a week, and Gross took the stand. Having done a postmortem examination on the victim, he was certain Mrs. Getter had been strangled. Gross described the research to date from the advanced medico-legal professionals in France on signs of asphyxiation by strangulation and explained how he'd arrived at his own conclusions with this same science. Gross had experimented on animals, strangling and dissecting them to examine the signs of manual asphyxiation. He believed this would confirm

Dr. Samuel Gross

his conclusions, but the medical experts for the defense said Margaret had died from apoplexy over stress from her strained relations with Getter. Thus, Getter was innocent.

Porter questioned Gross's approach and attacked him for failing to look at the victim's brain for a cause of death other than strangulation. Given the incomplete nature of his approach, Porter stated, how could he be so certain about his conclusions?

Undeterred, Gross stood by the new science. Porter brought in a dozen physicians to contradict young Gross, and they offered their diagnosis of apoplexy, but Dr. Gross stood his ground. Clearly, a good logical case could be made against Getter as well, and after only thirty-six minutes of deliberations, the jury found him guilty. He still protested his innocence, but a date was set for his hanging.

As the grim day approached, Getter confessed, affirming Dr. Gross's analysis. Gross went on to acquire a greater reputation in his field, once stating, "I have always thought the most important event of my professional life in Easton was the Getter trial." He went on to publish his work in *Observations on Manual Strangulation*, making his own contribution to the field of forensic science. Later he wrote another text, *Pathological Anatomy*, and developed a national reputation, as well as establishing a thriving practice in Philadelphia. He received a number of honorary degrees from universities abroad and founded the American Medical

Association. He also became the first president of the Medical Jurisprudence Society.

Getter, however, had a date with the gallows. When the day arrived, Easton took on a carnival atmosphere, as tens of thousands of people from around the countryside poured in to see the event. Getter donned a white suit and was escorted into the streets by Sheriff Daniel Robb. A procession of people accompanied them along the half mile to the tiny island in the Delaware where the gallows stood. The killer had to step across a series of boats strung together in a flotilla to get to the island.

Getters Island

Getter had requested to be hanged by a method different from the typical drop-and-break approach: He wanted to be drawn up and choked. So the rope was placed around his neck and then drawn up fast. He struggled for a few minutes before the rope broke, throwing him to the ground. "That was good for nothing," he said.

He had to wait, feeling the rope burn and contemplating his end for twenty-six minutes before a sturdier rope was found and brought to the island. To get on with it, he adjusted his scarf to hide the fresh mark on his neck. He then waited for the rope to tighten again. As Getter was lifted off his feet he struggled and kicked, and by some accounts, it took him fully eleven minutes to die. His body was left hanging for half an hour before it was removed for burial.

Three for the Money

Easton was the scene of yet another historic murder, a triple homicide in 1876 —possibly even a quadruple homicide. Fifty-seven-year-old Martin Laros, his wife, and six of his thirteen children lived on the Delaware in Mineral Spring, a hamlet of seven families located four miles north of Easton. They sat down to supper on the evening of May 30 with an older boarder, Moses Schug, who worked in Laros's furniture, undertaking and casket business. After a few bites, most of them felt the immediate onset of stomach cramps, and stumbled outside to the lawn to vomit. One of the younger girls, not as ill as the others, went to get their older brother, Clinton, who lived on his own. After Clinton arrived and saw that twenty-one-year-old Allen was assisting the others, he set out to fetch the local physician, who diagnosed poisoning as the cause. He administered emetics to produce more vomiting, but the victims all grew worse, complaining of a burning sensation.

The Fatal Family Supper (Image courtesy of NCGHS)

A second doctor arrived from Easton and he too tried to administer an antidote, but at 7:00 in the morning Mrs. Laros finally succumbed. She was the first to die, followed by her husband early that afternoon. The children were now all orphaned, and still quite ill. The next day, Moses Schug died.

Some of the suffering children reported that they had noticed a strange taste in the coffee, so the pot in which it was made was examined. At the bottom, mixed with the coffee grounds, was a heavy white sediment, indicative of arsenic. Indeed, after several tests involving a "blow-pipe," sulphate of copper, and the telltale arsenic mirror, it proved to be the toxic white powder, of a quantity sufficient to kill 100 adults. Yet the children held on. Allen Laros grew ill as well, but at a later hour than the others, so once the doctor had arrived, Allen took to his bed. Just before his mother's death, he went unconscious and was expected to die, but he revived. The physician noticed that Allen had never exhibited the deathly pallor the others had shown.

An investigation of the household indicated that the lock on Schug's personal trunk was broken, as was the lock on the secretary where Martin Laros kept his money. All of it—about $90—was "abstracted," as was $250 from the trunk. Suspicion fell on Allen, a local teacher who was currently studying law. "His character was known by many persons to be bad," wrote the *Times* reporter, and he was a reticent loner who apparently thought well of himself and was already suspected in earlier thefts from the household. Yet Allen had dined with the family and had also experienced a bad stomach-ache. If he was the poisoner, some people said, it seemed unlikely he would have partaken of coffee he knew was tainted.

Deputy Coroner H. S. Carey empanelled a coroner's jury of six men, calling as the first witness ten-year-old Alice Laros, now improved, who had prepared the coffee the night before. She had tasted it, but failed to notice anything wrong. Her older sister had filled the coffeepot with water and when she saw it turn white, she assumed there was leftover milk in it. She reported that the coffee had tasted "peppery." Both doctors testified before the jury, pointing out that Allen had been the person least affected. Clinton Laros described how Allen had been in bed since the incident, but had not once asked after the health and welfare of their parents.

However, Allen was now able to speak for himself. For the jury, he described what he had done on the fateful day after coming home from teaching. At dinner, his mother had commented that the beets tasted bad, but the others decided it was the coffee. Allen, who did not generally drink coffee, took two swigs, but did not like the taste. He said he hadn't noticed anything unusual about the household that evening and there were no strangers about. He knew that his father had put poison in the cellar to get rid of rats, but said he knew nothing about the symptoms of poison. He also described his own experience of the illness, interpreting his light symptoms as the result of taking only a brief taste of the tainted coffee. He did not count on the next person to testify.

A local pharmacist gave the most telling report. He said that a young man, who was acting nervous, had come to his shop on Monday that week to purchase rat poison in powder form. At first, this customer agreed to buy ten cents worth, but then asked for twenty-five cents. Finally, he wanted twice that amount. While this was not the only form of arsenic available, it was the only form he wanted. The pharmacist thought the encounter a bit strange, and he identified Allen C. Laros as the man who had purchased the arsenic. This incriminating circumstance seemed to close the case.

The coroner's jury returned a verdict of murder and identified Allen as the perpetrator. The police went to arrest him and at first he acted as if he was confused, but about ten minutes later, when they started to search the house, he blurted, "I done it." An officer and a juryman took his statement, which he signed on the spot. The *New York Times* published it in total, as did a reprint of an 1886 pamphlet, "The Laros Tragedy," sent to me by Nancy O'Hanlon, who first told us of the case.

The pamphlet offers a preface about the use of arsenic during this period for poisoning vermin and embalming the dead. "Anyone could and did easily obtain arsenic." Just four years earlier, the homicidal poisoning of Amanda Lucas in Bethlehem had been front-page news. The pamphlet's opening pages are filled with exaggerated language intended to inspire righteous rage against the defendant.

There's some indication from this account that Easton residents saw murder on a regular basis, but the poisoning of a "respectable, thrifty family" by a trusted member seemed beyond anyone's reckoning. "A sober, intelligent, fine-looking man turns out to be the infernal demon that coolly and deliberately planned and executed the cruel, heinous, devilish outrage."

1886 Pamphlet (courtesy of NCGHS)

It seemed stunning to many that Allen could sit at the table watching as each person drank a dose of poison that would send them retching to their beds and writhing in agony until they expired. "Is it possible for the 'human form divine' to descend to anything more brutal?" The pamphlet's author compared Laros to other heartless thrill killers of that era: fourteen-year-old Jesse Pomeroy, who murdered two children in Boston, mutilating the genitals of one; and church sexton Thomas Piper, the "Boston Belfry killer," who compulsively confessed to the slaying of a child and three women while under the influence of opium-inspired lust.

Accordingly, Allen described in his confession how he had come home from teaching, helped his mother, and then put arsenic into the coffeepot. He said he'd stolen the money from his father and Schug the evening before, hiding it in the yard, "between the privy and the sheep stable," beneath a board. As the coroner and constable dug it up, Allen added more details. He said that everyone needed to die so that he could spend the money as he pleased and admitted he'd stolen money from home on earlier occasions. He had also malingered being ill from the coffee. He would later claim he had only wanted his parents and siblings to become ill, not to die, because he was angry that his parents had refused to support him financially in his plan to study law.

Before he was taken to jail, Allen was allowed to see the corpses of his parents laid out in ice boxes inside the family home. He passed his hand downward over their faces and seemed intent on kissing their lips, but did not complete the act. At the corpse of Moses Schug he displayed no emotion. He asked his grieving siblings to pray for him, although his brothers admitted that they'd suspected him from the start. Three of the children had not yet recovered and the *New York*

15

Times reported that two of them could still die from ulcerations. One had already taken a turn for the worse.

In the coach on his way to the Northampton County prison, Allen admitted that his parents had always been good to him and he couldn't figure out why he had done this thing. At the prison, he requested a Bible.

This case, seemingly open-and-shut, became increasingly more intriguing to us, because there were suggestions in later articles that Allen Laros ended up a free man. It wasn't easy to piece the story together, but the following account is the result of our research.

Thousands of people came to the triple funeral or to gawk at the murder house. They followed the story with avid interest and then flocked to the trial. Two lawyers agreed to represent Laros, eyeing an insanity defense as their only recourse. By this time, questioning the *mens rea,* or mental state, had become a common strategy.

Despite the emphasis on free will in most criminal assaults, there were clear instances in which someone had acted from a delusional belief or a mental illness. Three decades earlier, in England, the 1843 M'Naghten ruling in the case of a delusional killer had laid out legal guidelines for England and America: to be legally insane, the accused must have been suffering from a disease or defect of the mind such that he was unaware of the nature of his act or unaware that what he was doing was wrong. Early psychiatry was just getting formalized in the mid-19th century and "alienists" were studying the criminally mentally ill. In 1837, the first psychotic man convicted of a criminal offense was paroled into an asylum, rather than prison. During the 1840s, psychiatrists discussed the limited range of behavioral control that such people had, publishing the first journals devoted to insanity to share case details with one another. They sought to understand the causes of homicidal insanity through a medical approach. It wasn't long before criminals, watching how the mentally ill avoided capital sentences, learned how to malinger a delusional psychosis.

Sitting in prison before his trial, Laros apparently had second thoughts about his actions and motives. He said he'd taken a sip of the coffee after seeing how sick the others got, so that he would die, too. He also mentioned he had been the first to propose getting a doctor so as to try to save the others, because he had not wanted them to die. The pamphlet says that Laros learned, while in prison, that his favorite brother had also died, which disturbed him, and it's the only suggestion in print that this incident might have been a quadruple homicide. During one interview, Allen cried over his lost family and stated that he'd assumed if he confessed, he'd be forgiven and would go to heaven. He said, "I was sane when I did it, am now, and if I had known it would result this way I would never have done it." He would eventually alter this position.

The trial commenced in August, two and a half months after the crime. Several doctors who examined Laros found that he suffered from epileptic seizures, but Dr. Traill Green testified for the prosecution to the effect that he had over forty patients who were epileptics and none was insane; aside from their periods of seizure, they lived healthy lives. Nevertheless, one of Laros's brothers described several epileptic episodes, including one so severe he had fallen on ice. A doctor for the defense stated he didn't think any of the family was "quite right," and research showed that Laros's paternal grandfather had actually been quite disturbed. He often did not know people familiar to him and had wandered away from home. His brother, too, was "of unsound mind." In addition, both grandmothers apparently had some kind of dementia and one of them had a brother who'd committed suicide. Thus, Allen had a family legacy of mental issues, and not long before the mass murder he'd threatened to kill himself. His mental condition became the principal mitigating factor, yet the fact that he'd stolen the money and purchased the arsenic in advance of the murders indicated a rational plan. He had known what he was doing.

On August 30, 1876, the jury convicted Allen Laros of intentionally murdering his father. Sentenced to be hanged the following September, he had his attorneys immediately request consideration of his mental instability. He experienced numerous epileptic seizures—as many as two a day—so by August 1877, the sentence was "respited," or postponed to determine if his problems warranted "humane treatment." The sheriff had been in the process of preparing the gallows when he learned that the hanging would not yet take place. It was rescheduled for October.

Laros had been epileptic since childhood, but the doctors who examined him were divided in their opinion of just how "crazy" he might be. Laros apparently wasn't happy about the delay. He "manifested considerable emotion," according to the *New York Times,* and one day he rigged up a device from the air register with his bed sheet to hang himself in his cell. The deputy warden found him, but managed to get him down before he died. He was "in the last stages of strangulation… In another moment he would have been dead." Once Laros was restored to consciousness, a guard was posted day and night to watch him.

The "Laros Commission" was appointed to investigate whether Laros was truly disturbed. There was concern in those days about hanging a man considered insane. Two physicians from Philadelphia, along with a doctor out of Doylestown, arrived to undertake the examination. While the details were not spelled out in the article, the doctors "did not see how any mortal man could stand without flinching the tests said to have been tried on Laros… during some of his spells." The Commission also questioned everyone in the prison with any contact with the prisoner, including the special watchman. During the hearing, Laros experienced a seizure, so the doctors examined him during it. They apparently decided he was "insane," or not competent to be executed, so in an unprecedented decision, Laros was moved to the State Insane Asylum in Harrisburg, Pennsylvania, and his capital sentence was suspended until he could be mentally restored. (A note: insanity now refers to the mental state at the time of the crime, not the present mental state during a trial or prior to execution; these are now competency issues. While both evaluations are based on mental stability and awareness, they refer to different issues. A defendant can be considered sane during the commission of a crime, but too psychotic to be subjected to the death sentence. In some cases, the defendant was found sane and convicted, but "went crazy" while awaiting execution.)

Asylums were not well-guarded in those days, and on at least three occasions Laros managed to escape. After one such incident, he got as far as Arkansas, taking odd jobs along the way, as documented in the *Easton Daily Express*. Oddly, he turned himself in, and apparently rejoiced that he could return to Easton for execution, for he "longed to die and be with my God." He did not even have to be manacled for transport. But while he adamantly resisted going back to the asylum, that's where he was taken. Laros believed he had too much sense to be confined with lunatics and disliked the way he was persecuted there. (During one stretch of freedom, he'd actually gone among yellow fever victims, either in the hope that he'd be listed among the dead and thus end the manhunt, or that he would contract the illness and die, as he believed that outright suicide would prevent him from getting into heaven.)

Laros apparently escaped again, and this time he disappeared. An uncorroborated report indicates that some time during the 1880s, a school in Texas inquired of the state of Pennsylvania whether an Allen C. Laros had a teaching permit. It's possible, then, that he found a job in Texas and no one was ever dispatched to bring him back. However, six years after the murders, the *Bucks County Gazette* printed an article to the effect that he had gotten married and officials from the "Lunatic Asylum" intended to go find him and bring him back to be hanged. There was some comment on how ineffective such places were at keeping people locked up and how little reason there seemed to have been to treat Laros as feeble-minded. Whatever became of him, no one around here knows, except that he apparently was never executed for the homicides.

The Laros decisions were later cited in an Oklahoma case about the execution of a mentally ill person, indicating that these justices had set a precedent. Since the guilt phase of the Laros trial had concluded, Laros had no right to having a jury hear the execution issue when it was raised at the conclusion of the trial. "The plea at this stage is only an appeal to the humanity of the Court to postpone the punishment until a recovery takes place." The standard was simple: whether the person about to be executed is aware of what this means and what he is about to suffer. The answer to that is, perhaps, not quite so simple, as it's an issue debated in the courts even today.

But speaking of precedents, the first recorded mob lynching in Pennsylvania occurred in Bethlehem.

Wild Justice

Thanks in part to how the Laros situation upset many residents, the first lynching in Pennsylvania occurred in Bethlehem in 1880. This involved a sexual offender whose lust for a child culminated in a gruesome double homicide. According to the account in the 1881 pamphlet, "Murder of the Geogles and the Lynching of the Fiend Snyder," shown to us by Colleen Lavdar of the Northampton County Historical and Genealogical Society (NCHGS) in Easton, the terrible incident occurred just after Christmas, on December 26. Jacob Geogle and his wife, Annie, had a home on the Monacacy Creek, about three miles north of Bethlehem. They had three girls, ages 11 to 14. Jacob, 38, worked in the ore mines. To help make ends meet, they had taken in a boarder, twenty-four-year-old Edward Snyder. This man developed a lust for the eldest daughter, Alice, and on several occasions he tried to accost her. She told her parents, who warned Snyder to stay away from her. But Snyder was not a man to be ordered about. Nor did he have any sense of decency. By all reports, he would stop at nothing to get what he wanted.

Like serial killer John Gacy, who dressed as a clown to entertain children, Snyder apparently donned the outfit of Santa Claus (*Belsnickel*) that Christmas to make the neighbors laugh, even as he plotted his revenge on the Geogles. The house was crowded on Christmas Day as the Geogles entertained another couple, the Youngs, with their two young daughters, inviting them to spend the night. Even this did not deter Snyder. That evening he sang hymns with the children and then went to his bed—a cot in the hallway. After the others were all settled, the Geogles retired to their bedroom. Alice and the oldest Young girl had a bedroom upstairs to themselves.

During the night, Snyder quietly rose, lit a candle, and placed it in the kitchen, which was next to the Geogles' bedroom. He took an axe from the woodpile (this was the age of axe murders around the country) and opened the door. Jacob snored in his place closest to the wall. Snyder stood near the bed and lifted the axe, bringing it down with such force that he cracked Jacob's skull. Synder repeated this with Annie. Then he proceeded to chop them up, spattering blood all over himself, the bed, the floor, and the walls. According to the pamphlet, "the mouths of both were cut nearly to the ears, and the necks were cut by repeated blows until the heads were nearly severed from the bodies." Snyder placed the axe across the bodies and went into the kitchen to remove his bloody shirt.

He then proceeded to the room where Alice was sleeping, intent on satisfying his lust. However, Alice was a strong girl and she screamed and fought him off. In the struggle, Snyder left behind bloody handprints, which would be evidence against him. One of the younger Geogles children ran to fetch her parents, but found their mutilated bodies instead. As she went back up the steps, Snyder seized the three younger girls and locked them in the bedroom with the two older girls before exiting the house. He took refuge in the nearby home of an acquaintance named George Ritter, telling him that four burglars had entered the Geogles house and slaughtered them. Snyder claimed he'd fought with them, but they'd left through a window.

In the meantime, the children had broken out of the room (no mention of what the Youngs were doing), and men came to find the bodies (perhaps called by Ritter). Snyder mingled among them, "cool" and indifferent, as they expressed horror over what they found and vowed vengeance on the murdering fiend. Apparently no one placed much stock in the tales told by children, because Alice pointed to the culprit and described his attempt to rape her, but when no one apprehended him he managed to slip away.

George Ritter and George Young reported the incident to the local magistrate, who sent for the coroner and district attorney. Detective W. W. Yohe, who worked for the railroad, arrived as well, and he would play the most prominent role in what was to come.

As word spread of what had happened, people started to come to the house to gaze at the gory mess. (In those days, no one thought about corrupting a crime scene.) However, "few persons remained in the presence of the dead longer than an instant." Unbelievably, Snyder remained in the vicinity, mixing with people and repeating his absurd story about the quartet of burglars. Yet his calm demeanor raised suspicions (apparently in a way that the children's story had not). Finally, two parties of five men each, armed with clubs and pitchforks, went looking for him. Yohe took charge and they soon came across Snyder hiding in the straw in Ritter's barn. As he jumped from the loft to the ground, some from the group yelled, "Hang him!" and "Cut his throat!"

Snyder was marched straight to the Geogles house, where the bodies still lay in bed, and was subjected to an inquest. There, he admitted he'd done it. A number of people mentioned how much it would cost in taxes to put him through a trial, and they recalled how Allen Laros, over in Easton, got a deal with an insanity ruling. They worried that Snyder might get away with murder. One man found a bed cord inside the home and brought it out to use, but Detective Yohe insisted on keeping Snyder alive for the DA. By now, the swelling crowd was calling for blood. They locked Yohe in the death chamber and dragged Snyder outside to a nearby chestnut tree.

Someone wrapped the cord around his neck, but no one was willing to climb the tree and drape it over a branch. Yohe, now free, stuck his hand between the cord and Snyder's neck, daring anyone to proceed. Snyder continued to admit his deed, saying to Yohe, "I'm not afraid to die. I deserve to for what I have done. The old man and me had words some time ago and I said I would fix him and I always keep my word. I am glad I killed them, and would do the same thing over. I want to talk to you a minute and all I ask those devils is that they will wait until I get through."

But no one was about to give this killer any consideration. A young man, John Mack, scrambled up the tree to place the rope over a limb. Snyder walked calmly over, ready. Yohe tried to save him, but "half a hundred willing hands" seized the rope and pulled, yanking Yohe off the ground three or four feet as Snyder rose into the air, choking. After five minutes, they let go of the rope, and Snyder fell with a thud back to the ground. They re-hung him, leaving him in place for three-quarters of an hour. He finally died from strangulation. His body was removed and taken to the county poorhouse, although it's not clear where he was finally buried.

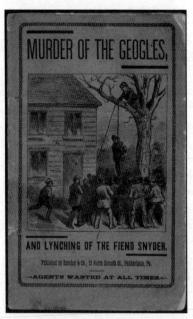

Geogles Murder Booklet
(Image courtesy of Helen P. Mack and Lehigh University's Digital Scholarship Center)

The DA wanted everyone directly involved to be arrested, but the local consensus was that no jury would convict anyone for this night's work. The prints of Snyder's bloody hands on the bed and sheets where he'd attacked Alice were sufficient evidence for his guilt, along with his uncoerced confession. "Lawyers should not get the devil off, as they did with Laros," the pamphlet's author writes, referring to the insanity ruling that had sent Laros to a psychiatric institution. He called it the "age of petted and pampered criminals." To set society aright after such an awful act, "severe cases ofttimes require severe remedies." In this incident, at any rate, the citizens of Bethlehem had lost faith in the machinery of justice, and the writer opined that the death penalty would be more effective as a deterrent if there was no board of pardons and no legal loopholes for killers to exploit.

Ghost stories soon grew up around the Geogles house and the chestnut tree, and as hundreds of people filed through the death chamber over the next few days, souvenir hunters stripped the hanging tree of all its twigs and branches. There was no mention of what happened to the children, but presumably they went to live with relatives.

No Place for a Child

The first man to be executed in Lehigh County was Harry Johnson, 23, after he confessed to the murder of his four-year-old daughter, Bertha May. He'd married a young woman in 1889, but the marriage had ended badly. Bertha May was their first child, but their second died young. Harry could not support the family, which caused a great deal of tension between him and his wife. Eventually they broke up, but when Harry failed in his child support payments, his wife left Bertha May with him. Harry tried foisting her off on his mother, but that arrangement lasted only so long before he faced having to care for her himself. He lived in a livery stable—no place, he thought, for a child.

Having little recourse, he decided to drown her in the Lehigh River. After throwing her in one summer day, he watched until she sank out of sight. But the river didn't carry her away. Four days later, she was hauled from the water, and thanks to various rumors, the coroner soon arrested Harry Johnson. There were plenty of witnesses to say that Johnson's daughter, the same age as the corpse, had suddenly disappeared. He claimed he'd given the girl to a stranger and blamed that person for drowning her.

Johnson was tried and convicted of first-degree murder, after which he confessed to what he'd done, blaming it all on his wife. On August 7, 1894, as he sang his favorite hymn and smoked a cigar, Harry dressed up and went to the gallows to be hanged—the same gallows used to hang the Molly Maguires in 1877. He was buried in West End Cemetery.

Halloween Demise

At the turn of the 19th century, in 1899, there were five different sets of murder/suicides in Lehigh County, all of them between married or romantic couples. Alice Kern was the last victim, killed by her estranged husband George as she fled from a streetcar on November 10. He'd threatened to do so if she did not return to him at once, but she had ignored him. Within hours of his threat, he'd shot her and then turned the gun on himself.

But as strange as it may be to have five such incidents in a single year, the following tale is far more bizarre.

On October 30, 1903, Thomas Bechtel, waited in his cell at the Central Police Station in Allentown. That afternoon, the funeral for his sister, Mabel, had taken place and the DA had sent word that Bechtel could not attend. Mabel had been murdered and he was a suspect, but he nevertheless went into a rage. Two of his brothers, also suspects, were held in cells close by. In fact, the entire family would soon be prosecuted for the crime, despite their protestations of innocence.

It seems that Mabel, known to give out sexual favors for material goods, had accompanied Alois Eckstein, the fiancé her mother had picked, to Philadelphia, where he left her before returning alone to Allentown. After midnight she was brought back to the family's row home on Cedar Street by another man, David Weisenberger, whom she loved. Her body was found two days later in an alley by her house, bludgeoned with a sharp-bladed implement. There were three cuts to the front of her head and one to the back. Also, her eyes were bruised and her nose broken. Her mother, Catharine, blamed Weisenberger, who resided in South Bethlehem.

From blood evidence present on clothing and a rug in the home, the DA suspected that Thomas had accidentally killed Mabel while the family was arguing with her over the possibility she would run off with Weisenberger; they desperately needed her income from the silk mill. Allegedly, Thomas had hit Mabel, knocking her against a bureau. In this hypothetical scenario, the family then decided to stage the crime to resemble a stranger assault, so they hit her head postmortem with a hatchet and concealed her body in the home until dark. The next evening, they placed the corpse outside, where it was discovered. Their plan apparently didn't work, because murder charges were lodged against all of them.

As reported in the *New York Times*, Thomas Bechtel, 30, was a drinker and could be a dangerous man when intoxicated. He'd been rejected from joining the police force. After the funeral, several family members visited him in cell #2, across from the cell that held Eckstein, a material witness. Around 4:00 P.M., Bechtel called out to Eckstein, indicating he wished they could die together. Not long afterward, Eckstein heard a strange gurgle and he called out to Bechtel, but received no response.

When the police sergeant looked into Bechtel's cell and saw blood on the floor, he opened the door and found him lying on a bench, his throat cut and a knife lying near him on the floor. Bechtel was beyond recovery. The police could not account for how he had gotten the knife, but assumed that someone had smuggled it in to him. He was, in fact, the second person in this family to commit suicide, the first being an older sister. Their father had died from an illness the year before.

The trials for other family members—Catharine, the "aged mother"; Myrtha (or Mythra), the sister; and the two brothers, Charles and John—took place in 1904, and included some unique forensic science testimony. David Weisenberger, initially among the accused, was acquitted of all charges on January 12, and agreed to testify about what he might know. He mentioned that he'd suggested to Mabel that she leave home and return to school, which had upset her family, who relied on her income. Apparently Eckstein had begged Mabel to stop dating Weisenberger and had hit her, but Weisenberger had walked her home on the night she had disappeared, leaving her at her door.

Catharine Bechtel was tried first, in January. Supposedly, she knew what her daughter was doing with men and as long as it filled the family coffers, that was fine with her. The Commonwealth contended, with forty witnesses, that she had been an accessory after the fact, as well as a participant in the murder. (The siblings were all charged only as accessories after the fact.) Eckstein took the stand to say he'd been willing to marry Mabel, as arranged, despite knowing that she was loose with men. He'd gone to the Bechtel home on the day Mabel was supposedly murdered and said that the family had acted strangely, but he saw nothing suspicious.

Dr. John Lear, a biological expert from Muhlenberg College, had examined stains on a carpet in the Bechtel home using a recently discovered method of analysis. Two years earlier, Jules Bordet from Belgium had shown that a vaccination elicited a specific antibody and he could see a visible reaction between the antibody and an antigen. Others who injected animals against infectious diseases found that foreign substances elicited a defensive reaction in the blood. Biologist Paul Uhlenhuth then found that when injecting protein from a chicken egg into a rabbit and mixing serum from the rabbit with egg white, the egg proteins would separate from the liquid to form a precipitin. He also discovered that the blood of each animal had its own characteristic protein and that the test was applicable to humans. Thus, he had found a way to correctly state that suspicious blood stains originated with humans.

Dr. Lear, who followed his lead, stated that the blood stains from the Bechtel home were from a person, but the defense hired a chemistry professor, Dr. Alvin Davidson from Lafayette College, to contest the method as unproven. Lear admitted it was the first time the "Bordet method" had been used in a murder case in America, but he gave an exhaustive explanation of how it worked and affirmed its reliability. Cross-examination failed to discredit it. Two other doctors, one from Johns Hopkins University who complained that he was not being compensated, confirmed that the test was "absolute in its conclusions." With this, the prosecution rested its case.

Yet Catharine's attorney aimed not only to acquit his client, but to remove suspicion from her dead son, Thomas, as the murderer. As he cross-examined witnesses, he raised the issue more than once, hoping to plant in the minds of jurors the notion that suicide was not an admission of guilt. He also brought in more experts to refute the blood stain analysis. The "battle of the experts," as a reporter called it, continued as the attorney used six scientists to state that the Bordet test was unreliable. One even admitted he had never tried it. At this point, Judge Trexler instructed the jury to pay no attention to any witness, expert or not, who was not fully informed about the science of this test.

These experts went on to testify that the only item removed from the Bechtel home on which there was human blood was the undervest Mabel had worn when attacked. The attorney claimed that all other stains were probably tobacco or something from one of the family pets, and he argued that Mabel had been killed away from the house, not inside. He placed all members of the family on the stand to exonerate their mother, including Catharine herself. She testified for over four hours, during which time she denied, in a peculiar Pennsylvania Dutch dialect, that her son had killed Mabel or that he had guilty knowledge of the crime and cover-up. Under cross-examination, she could not be shaken into contradicting herself or admitting to anything. When asked if she knew how Mabel had died, she stated, "God knows that I don't. If I did know it I would not be here now. I would have said it long ago… I have often prayed and implored that it be revealed before I die."

Catharine's trial lasted nine days, and on January 23, once the jury went to deliberate, it took them only an hour to acquit her. As she was released from custody, she broke into tears. The trial of her children was postponed until April, at which time the jury was unable to render verdicts against any of the defendants, so the cases were all dropped. Eckstein, too, was acquitted of any wrongdoing (despite a history of abuse), so Mabel's murder went unsolved, although many people continued to believe that Thomas's suicide was a clear statement of guilt. What we do know in retrospect is that the blood test that was used was indeed reliable, so no matter how much Catharine Bechtel protested, there was certainly human blood on a rug in her house.

Thrown to the Pigs

In 1908, George N. Schaffer appeared to have been the last person to have seen itinerant jewelry salesman Leopold Ermann alive. When no one heard from him for over a week, Leopold's brother contacted the Allentown police and went looking for him. They ended up with a warrant to search Schaffer's chicken farm in Schnecksville, thanks to a tip from another farmer's wife. Schaffer, 24, acted nervous when they arrived and even as police took him in for questioning, another farmer with self-described psychic powers said he could "see" a body under the floor of Schaffer's pigsty.

In fact, the concrete floor had been recently poured, so investigators broke it up and started to dig. Sure enough, they found dismembered remains about two feet down, drawing thousands of curious people via salacious newspaper accounts to come have a look. The man had been killed with an ax, and apparently beheaded and cut into pieces with a butcher knife. His parts were then wrapped in a tattered quilt and dumped into the hole. It turned out that the beloved jeweler, a salesman for 25 years, had been friends with Schaffer.

After a three-day trial in June (with males on one side of the courtroom and females on the other), as criminalists discussed the possibility that Schaffer had been warped in the womb from his mother's emotional stress, the culprit was found guilty. Although he'd been distant throughout the proceedings, his response to the verdict was to fall to the floor in a dead faint. Just before he was set to hang in 1910, he confessed. According to records, he was the last person to be hanged in Lehigh County Prison. After that, the state switched to the electric chair.

Witches' Curse

Although this next homicide did not occur in the Lehigh Valley, it resulted from something penned by a Valley resident. Ned Heindel authored a book about

Hexenkopf, an area in Williams Township in which stories of demons and witches flourished for a time. John George Hohman, who resided there during the 19th century, penned *Der Lange Verborgene Freund* (*The Long Lost Friend*), printed in 1820, and it soon became a bible for occultists and faith healers. Supposedly, those who possessed this book gained power and protection, but apparently that didn't work out for Nelson Rehmeyer over near York, Pennsylvania. It seems that a rival witch-doctor, John Blymire, was feeling under the weather for quite a while, and had suffered a series of setbacks. He learned from another witch-doctor that Rehmeyer was the cause. To gain relief, Blymire would have to burn Rehmeyer's copy of the Hohman book of spells, or get a lock of his hair and burn that. Just after midnight on November 28, 1928, Blymire and two accomplices entered Rehmeyer's home, murdered him, hacked up his body, and burned it. They were arrested and tried. All three were convicted, receiving sentences of various lengths, but eventually all were paroled. The case drew national attention because of the witchcraft connection, despite the fact that the judge refused to allow anything dealing in black magic to be mentioned during the proceedings.

Hex Murder Book

Around the same time as this trial, a high profile murder occurred back in the Valley.

The Socialite

Frank Whelen used to write an occasional column in the *Morning Call* about historic events from around the Valley. One of these featured an incident involving the wife of a well-to-do insurance broker, Roy van Wagenen of Allentown. They lived in the West End and owned a stylish Hudson Coupe. During August 1929, just after they had dined at the local country club, something terrible happened to Emile van Wagenen.

On August 18, she was found unconscious near 29th and Liberty. Although she still wore her pearls and diamonds, her purse was missing. Taken to a hospital, she remained unconscious for several days as doctors treated her head wound, but she finally died on August 23. Without leads or witnesses, there was no way to investigate, aside from asking questions about the nature of this woman's relationship with her husband.

But then in September, three boys offered a provocative story. On the night in question, at around 9:10 P.M., they had seen a maroon Hudson Coupe, license number 18-369, traveling slowly near 29th and Liberty. Suddenly the car lights went out and the passenger side door opened. They saw a woman's legs come out onto the running board and she seemed to have been pushed out to the street. Oddly, rather than assist her, they followed the coupe, noting that the driver was a man. He'd driven about a mile and then turned on the car lights again. These young men told enough people about this incident that it eventually got back to the district attorney. He sent detectives to arrest Roy van Wagenen. The broker seemed less surprised than annoyed that they had come during his busy time and he asked why they couldn't wait; he wasn't going anywhere. Despite the fact that the witnesses had reported Roy's license plate number, most of his acquaintances believed he'd been wrongly accused.

Yet Roy gave conflicting stories about his whereabouts that night. He gave two different times for his departure from the Lehigh Valley Country Club on August 18, only one of which gave him an alibi for the time the young men saw the coupe. His trial started on September 30. Many witnesses defended him, saying they had seen the couple that day and there was nothing amiss. Roy had decided to return home early, leaving his wife at the club.

A bit of science was introduced for Roy's defense. Experts described how wind resistance would have made it impossible for Roy, driving at 25 MPH, to have opened the car door and pushed a person to the street, putting into doubt what the three young men claimed to have seen. In fact, a physician said that Roy suffered from such bad rheumatism he could not have managed it. Roy took the stand himself to endure cross-examination. He claimed that his wife had not been in his car that entire week, let alone that night. He insisted he did not throw her out. Despite the DA's attempt to shake his story, he repeated what he'd said. In closing, the DA reminded the jurors that the witnesses had described van Wegenen's car and even had the license number right. Yet these citizens declined to convict. Roy van Wagenen was declared not guilty, and he went home, soon to suffer the reversal of fortune that most of the rest of the country experienced during the catastrophic failure of the stock market the following month.

Mystery in the Colonnade

Where the Wachovia bank now stands on 54 West Broad Street, near Getter, was once the location of the Colonnade nightclub. On November 10, 1949, a woman was found dead in the basement of the building. Ruth Mickley, a thirty-one-year-old club hostess, turned up on the couch in the bar area known as the Rumpus

Room. A utility man found the body around 6:00 A.M., although he did nothing because he thought she was merely sleeping. However, someone later reported the body to the police. A Northampton County coroner's jury listened to stories from the Colonnade's owner, a band leader, a waitress, and three employees of Lehigh Surgical Steel, deciding that Mickley had been hit with a blunt instrument. It looked like a case of murder until the DA suddenly announced on December 6, that there had been no homicide at all. Mickley had merely fallen down the stairs and hit her head. He based this on the fact that lie detector tests had been given to all the suspects and they came up clean. Thus, there were no suspects. How Mickley had ended up on the couch was never explained. Nor was the reliance of a public official on such poor logic. Just because identified suspects fail to pan out does not prove there are no suspects; it could be a flaw in the investigation, or that a person at the club killed Mickley and left, with no one the wiser as to his or her identity.

The following year, the Colonnade closed its doors and the building next housed a bank branch, just as it does today.

The Colonnade

We now leave behind the historical crimes and move into the most common type of violence: family murders.

PART II: DOMESTIC DISTURBANCE

Around 70–75% of homicides are situational, i.e., they arise from within a situation of tension, such as domestic turmoil or anger at a friend or associate. The Valley has its share of people who killed someone they knew—perhaps even once loved—and among these crimes are a few that got national attention. We can't begin to cover all such stories, but we've made what we think is an intriguing selection.

The Body in the Rug

When I first moved to the Valley in the summer of 2001, I was living near Hellertown, and within a month, a body was found rolled up inside a rug in the basement of a former jewelry store on Main Street. New owners cleaning out the space had come across it. In fact, the remains were pretty decomposed, but it wasn't difficult to identify the victim and link her to the culprit, because only one person had access to the building in which the rug had been deposited. Alton Field, 51, had told the police two years earlier in May 1999, when his fifty-six-year-old wife, Teresa, went missing, that she had run off with another man in the middle of the night.

Main Street Hellertown

At the time, Field was living in South Whitehall Township. The couple had been married for 32 years. Neighbors claimed they'd seen another woman at the Field home, suggesting a motive for murder. Teresa's mother had also informed police that her daughter's clothing was still in the home and a large rug was missing. It turned out that a family friend had helped Field remove the rug, which he said had been unusually heavy. Neighbors apparently had seen the rug being carried out as well, and police who searched the home discovered a mattress turned upside down. On the underside were red stains. Yet despite these suspicious circumstances, the investigation was apparently dropped, because Teresa was nowhere to be found.

After an examination of the remains from the rug, Coroner Zack Lysek said the victim had died from blunt force trauma to the head. Field was charged with one count of criminal homicide and held in the Northampton County prison. Since the body had been found in Northampton County, that's where the prosecution took place.

In June 2004, Alton Field went to trial in Easton. He admitted killing his wife in their bedroom on May 26, just as the evidence showed, but he said it was self-defense. She had wielded a baseball bat at him and after he took it from her, she reached for a gun, so he bludgeoned her to save himself. Uncertain what to do next, he'd wrapped her battered body in a rug and taken it to his jewelry store in Hellertown. There it lay for two years. He apparently forgot about it when he sold the store. During the trial, it came out that Alton and Teresa had marital problems. A year before her death, he'd started an "internet affair" with another woman. Thus, he had motive to want Teresa out of the way.

Field's defense attorney, Robert Patterson, argued that the jury should be offered the possibility of convicting Field of manslaughter, but Judge Robert Freedberg said there was no evidence of either heat-of-the-moment or self-defense. He declined to give the jury this alternative. It did not much matter, because after they returned a verdict of first-degree murder for a life sentence, the jury foreman told reporters that no one had believed Field's story of Teresa attacking him. The degree of damage done to her head had seemed the result of a force greater than an act of self-defense would indicate.

Such incidents often result from triangulated relationships, but the next one had sufficient complications to fill a book—and did.

Justice for Devon

A love triangle in Easton ended in the death of one of the parties, nineteen-year-old Devon Guzman. On June 15, 2000, her body was found, with her throat slashed, in a car in a parking lot at the Delaware Canal State Park. Her dirt-smudged clothing bore animal hair from both a cat and dog, which was collected for comparison should a suspect develop. An investigation soon linked Devon with a married couple, Michelle Hetzel, 20, and Brandon Bloss, 26. Investigators learned that Michelle was having an affair with Devon and it didn't take much intelligence to grasp what led to the fatal violence: a tangle of relationships flavored by jealousy and possessiveness. The couple had a cat and dog with fur consistent with the hairs found on Devon. In addition, a bite mark on Brandon's arm appeared to be consistent with Devon's teeth imprints.His clothing from the trunk of Michelle's car bore spots of Devon's blood. With this clothing were two pair of bloodstained rubber gloves.

Although Brandon and Michelle had different attorneys, they were tried together. However, since the trial began in September 2001, the 9-11 terrorist attacks on the World Trade Center and Pentagon caused a mistrial. Jurors were too upset to continue, although DA John Morganelli had already made his opening statement: Devon was killed because she was interfering with the defendants' marriage.

According to the story that was pieced together, on June 14, Devon told her roommate she was going to the home of Brandon and Michelle, but Michelle called later to say that Devon had never arrived. Michelle and the roommate went to search for Devon and discovered her car in the park. When they saw her body, an apparent suicide, they called the police. However, the coroner found that Devon had not died in the car; she had been killed elsewhere and placed there. Her throat was cut too deeply to have been self-inflicted and there was insufficient blood in the car.

According to the book, *Lipstick and Blood*, Michelle, Devon, and Devon's roommate had been high school friends. Michelle had married Brandon, while Devon moved in with the other girl. Michelle then used her husband's credit card to fly, with Devon, to St. Croix to get secretly married. Later, when Devon wanted to break up, Michelle had been upset. They had a series of arguments and after one, Devon was found dead.

With a new jury in place, the trial continued. Michelle testified that she'd had nothing to do with the murder, because she was in love with Devon. She added that her husband (who did not testify) had confessed. Brandon's attorney pointed the finger back at Michelle, acknowledging only that Brandon had assisted in taking the body to the park. But an acquaintance of theirs said on the stand that two months before the homicide, Michelle had asked *him* to kill Devon, which belied her claim to have loved the girl. Other witnesses said that the night before the killing, Michelle had fought with Devon, because she refused to leave her other lover (the roommate). Michelle admitted to having an argument, but she said it had been about how the relationship was putting a strain on her marriage. Michelle's mother threw the spotlight back on Brandon when she testified that he'd been angry over the affair and had threatened to kill Devon several times.

By October 4, the jury was in deliberations and the next day they reached a verdict: both parties were guilty of first-degree murder. Thus, both received life in prison.

Brandon appealed on the grounds that the prosecution had erroneously relied on photographs taken by a forensic odontologist, at his own attorney's behest, of the bite mark on his arm. They should instead have used the photographs taken by the investigators. In 2003, the Pennsylvania Superior Court agreed that the photographs were "work product," and therefore protected. However, the error was deemed "harmless," because there was an overwhelming amount of independent evidence with which to convict.

Michelle appealed as well, but her argument about the inflammatory nature of the crime scene photos was denied. Both made a bid for a new trial, which was denied in 2007. Now divorced, Michelle and Brandon claimed they had not been apprised of their right to present character witnesses, although the records contradict this. They will probably continue to seek a new trial.

It's not just love that troubles relationships; sometimes it's just the fact of being related. Our next case was a shocker throughout the Valley, and because the offender was a juvenile, we have changed the name.

The CSI Effect

Around noon, twelve-year-old John shot his mother in the face with a Remington .22-250-caliber rifle. She died instantly. John ran outside to tell his sisters and one of them ran to get a neighbor. According to initial reports, John told the police that an intruder had entered the home and killed his mother. However, his grandparents, who arrived later, insisted he tell the truth, so he admitted he'd removed the gun from a cabinet in the backyard shed and took it into the house where his mother was talking on the phone. John's father was away at work at the time, but when questioned he insisted he kept his hunting rifles unloaded and under lock and key. He had one of only two keys with him and believed his wife had hidden the other. The implication was that John had discovered the hidden key and unlocked the cabinet. But he added that John had learned how to properly use a gun.

John claimed he'd merely wanted to handle the rifle and had not known it was loaded. He'd taken it into the house to show his mother, where it had accidentally gone off, shooting her in the face as she sat on the couch talking on the phone. Yet the spent cartridge was found outside in the backyard rather than in the house, and the gun had been replaced in the cabinet. Thus, it appeared to be something other than an accident.

Factors that came out of the investigation shed a more negative light. First, the lab results indicated that John had held the gun inches from his mother's face when he shot her (although a blood spatter analysis of his clothing said it was farther away). Also, he'd used her key to get into the shed, his fingerprints were on an ammunition box, and he'd locked his sisters in the shed. In other words, he'd not discovered the gun loaded, but had loaded it himself. Why his sisters had been locked in the shed was a mystery. It was time to examine John's past record.

A psychological assessment indicated that John had no identifiable mental illness but had "gun-related issues." He'd been violent in the past, as well as deceptive. When he was ten, his mother had denied him permission to go on a fishing trip, so he took the family's van, crashed it and claimed he'd been kidnapped. He'd shot a neighborhood girl with a BB gun, pointed it at other children, and placed a gun of some kind against the head of a boy at Bible camp.

John's father was largely absent during the week, so John's mother had ruled a strict household, home-schooling all three children. John had bristled at his mother's control. Regardless of how he felt, evidence revealed at least part of the truth: After shooting his mother, John walked outside, ejected the spent cartridge in the yard, unlocked the shed and told his sisters their mother was dead. A neighbor who assisted them said the girls were shaken, but John had exhibited no emotion whatsoever. He quickly lied to police about what happened, but the person to whom his mother had been speaking on the phone contradicted what he said. John claimed he had told his mother about the gun and she had asked him to wait a minute. In fact, she had stopped talking in mid-sentence and no such conversation had taken place.

Opinions about what happened were mixed. John remained in detention for several years, and as he went through the juvenile system, he reportedly learned better anger management skills.

John's not the only young man to have decided that the solution to family issues is violence. Our next two cases are more horrendous yet.

The Skinhead Murders

The scene at the middle-class house on the border of Allentown, in Salisbury Township, was unthinkable. Everyone who saw the carnage that day, Tuesday, February 27, 1995, was stunned: Three of the five members of the Freeman family lay in various areas of the house, bludgeoned and stabbed.

Dennis Freeman, 54, had been head custodian at a local high school, and his wife Brenda, 48, a homemaker. They'd been devout Jehovah's Witnesses, raising their three boys to abide by strict rules: no birthdays, celebration of national holidays, voting, or military service. Yet their two teenage sons had grown into rather large and belligerent boys. Bryan, 17, stood six feet tall, weighed 215 pounds, and had an interest in a military career. David, at 15, was six-foot-three and weighed a hulking 245 pounds.

Brenda confided to acquaintances that she was afraid of them because they had threatened to kill her and Dennis. Even from a young age the two brothers were distressing. David disliked the religious restrictions on extracurricular activities in which his friends freely participated, and both boys stopped attending church services. Shortly after David joined the school football team, he was suspended for threatening the coach, and was then committed to rehab for substance abuse. Released, he was still a handful, so he was sent to a hospital, where doctors recommended he be admitted to a residential placement facility. A psychiatric evaluation found him to be intelligent, but at risk for developing antisocial personality disorder.

Bryan was reportedly smarter than his younger brother, and more polite. He even made the school honor roll. Yet he, too, experimented with drugs and was sent to a treatment facility. There he joined the skinheads, which seemed to give him a sense of purpose. He decorated his room with swastikas and images of Hitler. White people, Bryan learned from this hate organization, were the descendants of Abel, the good and noble son of Adam and Eve, while others were sons of the despicable Cain.

Bryan Freeman

Upon Bryan's return home, he got David—just back, himself—involved with the skinheads. They decided to form their own neo-Nazi group with a cousin, Benny Birdwell. All three shaved their heads, got tattoos, and proclaimed their loyalty to the white supremacy movement. Bryan was angry that his parents had placed him in what he viewed as a "mental institution" and he decided he would show them who was boss.

Brenda sought help from the Anti-Defamation League of the B'Nai Brith, supposed experts on cult behavior. They sent her to an anti-prejudice coordinator, but she received little help. She had also tried Toughlove, a group for parents with difficult children, and the Pennsylvania Human Relations Commission, but no one seemed to have an answer. Dennis reportedly kept a baseball bat by their bed for protection.

On February 4, 1995, Brenda sold her sons' cars, and the next day they tattooed their foreheads, David with "Sieg Heil" and Bryan with "Berzerker." In reaction, Brenda and Dennis went through their rooms and removed the hate paraphernalia. These actions only made the brothers angry and they told friends they were going to steal a gun.

Young Erik, trapped in this house, sensed what was coming. When his aunt asked him how he was getting along with his brothers, he said, "You never know when you're going to die." He asked her to look after his dog. Not long afterward, she would find him bludgeoned to death in his bed.

Officer Michael Pochran was the first to respond to the scene, discovered by the aunt, and he quickly called for back-up. In the dining room, resting against a cabinet, they found a bloodstained aluminum bat. From there, they went to the master bedroom, where they discovered Dennis Freeman, his face and head smashed so badly that his brain was exposed. His throat was slashed as well. The officers proceeded to Erik's room where they already knew they would find their second victim, and then looked for Brenda. On the basement stairs lay a metal pipe covered with blood and on the floor was Brenda, lying on her side in her nightgown, with a bloody knife next to her. She had been bludgeoned and stabbed. On a wall behind her body were two crudely drawn swastikas.

There was no one else in the home. Both David and Bryan were missing, along with the family's Sunbird. There seemed little doubt as to who the perpetrators were. Yet it soon became clear that a third party was involved: their cousin, Nelson "Benny" Birdwell III. The hunt was on to find them.

A truck driver who had heard about the murders on the radio gave the police their best lead, pointing them toward Truck World Motor Inn in Hubbard, Ohio, just over the Pennsylvania/Ohio border. A videotape from a nearby grocery had caught the image of three boys inside the store and they were soon located at the home of a skinhead associate in Michigan. They were arrested but remained in Michigan for the moment.

David offered one rendition of events: He reported that they had all gone out to dinner and then to the movies. David went to *Murder in the First*, while the other two saw *Boys on the Side*. When they returned home around 10:30 P.M., Brenda was waiting. She asked Benny to leave. He obeyed, but then crawled back in through the window. Brenda and Bryan began to yell at each other and Bryan attacked her. He then told the others they had better not "puss out" or they would get stabbed, too. He ordered David and Benny to go upstairs and kill Dennis and Erik. David said that he had killed them both and that Benny had taken money, but had not participated in the actual slaughter.

Benny had a version, too. He described the trip to Wendy's and the theater, and said that Brenda had ordered him several times to go home. Yet he'd always come back in through a window. Then Brenda and Bryan got into a fight and Bryan ran into his room, obtained a steak knife, and came back out. Brenda tried to run, but Bryan caught her and placed his hand over her mouth, thrusting the knife into her back. Brenda fell to the floor, but soon got back up, pulled the knife from her back and advanced on her son. Bryan and Brenda struggled for the knife, but he

"Benny" Birdwell III

regained control and stabbed her once more in the shoulder all the way up to the hilt. She tried to scream, but he stuffed a pair of shorts into her mouth so their father would not hear. Finally, she lay still.

When they had finished her off, they knew they had to kill Dennis and Erik. Birdwell said he remained in the basement while the brothers did the dirty work. Once Dennis and Erik were dispatched, Bryan yelled for Benny to come upstairs, so he did. Bryan, he saw, was covered in blood. Getting into the family car with around $200 from Dennis's billfold, they argued about where to go and then fled to their friend's farm in Michigan. On the way, they discussed returning to make the whole thing look like it had been the work of an intruder, bent on robbery, but they were too late: on the radio they heard about the discovery of the triple homicide. So they kept going.

Donna Birdwell, Benny's mother, was outraged that her son had been forced into this situation, so she told a reporter for the *Midland Daily News* what Benny had said. The Freeman brothers read the article and realized that Benny was throwing the entire blame on them. Angry, they decided to retaliate. Bryan had yet to say anything, and now he was ready. He and David asked for attorneys and offered to tell the whole truth and nothing but the truth.

Bryan required several conditions before they would make formal statements. He wanted the death penalty taken off the table, he and his brother would not give up their right to a trial, and they wanted to give an interview to a reporter of their choice. The deal was approved by Allentown prosecutor Robert Steinberg.

35

On March 6, the same day on which Dennis, Brenda, and Erik were laid to rest in a cemetery in Allentown, David sat down with an attorney and several police officers who had arrived from Pennsylvania. Admitting he'd lied at first to protect his cousin, he described once again how they had spent the evening and how Bryan had stabbed Brenda. He added that he and Benny had gone upstairs together to Dennis's room. Benny had a pickax handle with him and David had grabbed an aluminum bat out of the hallway closet. They had then argued quietly over who would strike the first blow. He said that Benny did it and had cut Dennis's throat as well. David admitted to hitting his father four times in the face, but said that Benny was the one who had killed Erik, cracking his skull. Benny had told them that Erik's eye popped out of his head.

Bryan was next, going over some of the same territory, but closing up holes, especially with his own involvement in his mother's murder. He said that after he killed his mother, Benny was still downstairs with him and had used the handle of a pick ax to hit her over the head. Then he went upstairs to help David. Bryan claimed that Benny had told him that he'd hit both Dennis and Erik in the face and had stated that he'd shattered Erik's skull. Bryan denied that he'd instructed the other two to go kill the rest of the family. He also denied that he'd ever threatened his parents. Taking the rap for Benny, he said, was Benny's idea, because Bryan's stint in a mental institution might help him mitigate the crime.

Bryan, David, and Benny went before a Michigan judge to hear a formal reading of the charges against them: three counts of first-degree murder, while Benny was also charged with hindering apprehension. They all agreed to extradition.

In Allentown again, the three offenders were taken to a prison facility in Lehigh County. The brothers received no bail, but Birdwell was held on $250,000 bail. His parents hired attorney Richard Makoul. Bryan was assigned Allentown public defenders Earl Supplee and Jim Netchin. They hoped that he might testify against his brother, thought to be the principal instigator, to avoid excessive jail time. Judge Lawrence Brenner assigned David's case to Wally Worth and Brian Collins, who set to work to get him transferred to the juvenile court.

Steinberg reviewed the statements the boys had made, and when he spotted several significant inconsistencies, he decided the brothers had lied: the deal was made on the condition they told the truth and they had violated it. Steinberg called the deal off and announced he would accept a plea of first-degree murder from any of the defendants, but if they chose to go to trial, he would recommend death. Steinberg was nevertheless convinced that Benny, the principal troublemaker, had killed Erik and beaten Dennis.

At the arraignment, Lehigh County Coroner Isidore Mihalakis testified first. He believed that Dennis had been struck first, approximately six times on the head and seven to the chest, fracturing the ribs and breastbone. He also had found a superficial cut along Dennis's neck and fractures to his nose, eye sockets, and left jaw. The brain had come through a four-inch fracture of the forehead, and he'd been hit three to five times in the face with two different weapons. To the coroner, this indicated two attackers in that room. Dennis had died from the extreme head injuries.

Mihalakis then reported that Brenda had died from blood loss. There was a stab wound to the tip of her right shoulder that had gone at least five inches deep and a stab wound to her right scapula that went through her lung and into her heart, causing blood leakage into the chest. In addition, he'd counted eight blows to the head, one of which had been to the back.

Erik bore several blunt force injuries to his forehead, the left side of his face, his left arm, and the back of his hands. His brain, too, had protruded from one wound. There were injuries to his face and head, including bruises and lacerations. His hands were fractured and his left forearm bruised, indicating that he may have tried to defend himself from the blows. Erik died from head injuries caused by an aluminum bat.

Steinberg offered Benny a plea of murder one, with the death penalty off the table. Benny refused it, maintaining his innocence. Then, on July 24, David's lawyers claimed that he had been suffering from mental infirmity at the time of the crime and they were prepared to plead insanity on his behalf. In addition, the public defenders for both brothers filed papers regarding Steinberg's failure to keep to the terms of the plea deal. They stated that when he'd offered the confession, Bryan had relied on the Michigan authorities to do things properly. It was not his fault they hadn't. In addition, David's attorneys insisted that the death penalty for a 15-year-old was cruel and unusual punishment (and in 2005, the Supreme Court agreed). They also stated that when he'd confessed, David had been under the influence of narcotics.

But then something happened to shift the case. On July 27, the Pennsylvania State Crime Lab announced a finding that supported the brothers' version of events. Blood spatter found on the T-shirt that Birdwell had worn that night was a match to Dennis Freeman. Thus, the story Birdwell had told was clearly false, because he'd been in the room when Dennis was under attack, standing close enough for blood spatter to hit him.

Steinberg grabbed this important bit of evidence and commended the scientists. He then charged Birdwell with three counts of first-degree murder. Along with Coroner Mihalakis' belief that three weapons involved implicated three separate killers, he pieced together a scenario that made logical sense: Bryan had stabbed his mother, while David and Benny had gone together to kill Dennis and Erik. He also believed that Benny had slammed Brenda with the same pickax handle that had been used on Erik: it bore traces of blood from both. While Erik's blood was not found on anyone's clothing, a hair consistent with his was picked off a jersey that Bryan had worn that night. In any event, there was good reason to believe that Birdwell had been every bit as involved in this triple homicide as the two brothers.

Makoul quickly countered that being present in the room where Dennis was being killed did not prove that Birdwell had acted. It could even show that he was

37

trying to stop the murder. But Birdwell's obvious lies did not help matters; had he been trying to help the victims, he'd have said so. Steinberg announced that he intended to convict the boys separately, because he could use the statements each had given against any of the others.

Investigators turned up stories about how much the boys had hated their parents. Todd Reiss, who had been in Lehigh County Prison with Benny, said that Benny had admitted he'd helped Bryan kill Brenda. Benny had also allegedly stated that the murders had been planned, but his description of the crime had changed: in this version, he'd allegedly distracted Brenda so that Bryan could attack her from behind. He said that Dennis and Erik had been killed first (as the coroner had believed), and that Brenda had been the most difficult to kill.

Lehigh County Courthouse

On November 14, the attorneys for all three defendants argued in court that Steinberg had reneged on his agreement. Judge Brenner urged Steinberg to make another deal, but he resisted. He thought he had a good case. But Michigan-based skinhead Frank Hesse was there to testify that David had been drunk and high on marijuana prior to his arrest. That placed his competency to confess into doubt. The judge took all of this into consideration and said that he would give his ruling at a later date.

Then on December 7, Bryan surprised everyone: He admitted in court that he had murdered his mother. He received a life sentence and would not have to testify against his brother or cousin. David notified his lawyers that he wanted the same deal, and a week later, despite their cautions against it, he was in court for the same reason. He admitted that he had killed his father, but said he did not know why.

Judge James Diefenderfer presided over the murder trial for Nelson Benjamin Birdwell III. He did not allow any testimony about Benny's skinhead involvement, which took some of the force out of Steinberg's argument. Makoul's strategy was to show that Benny had an IQ of 78, which made him borderline mentally retarded. In addition, after the murders he had suffered from acute anxiety disorder, which had fueled his decision to accompany his cousins to Michigan.

Steinberg insisted that Benny had been an active participant in the murders, as indicated by the blood spatter on his shirt and by statements in the Freeman brothers' confessions. Makoul pointed out that Benny was mentally retarded, a follower, and had happened to walk into the master bedroom when David had swung the weapon that had killed Dennis Freeman.

The crime lab technician testified about the DNA procedure that had determined that Dennis Freeman's blood was found on Benny's T-shirt. She said the drops could not have traveled very far, so he had to have been close when the impact was made. To test this, Dr. Barbara Rouley had covered wood with a thin layer of horse blood and plastic. She hit the wood with a baseball bat and observed how far the blood spattered, and then analyzed patterns that appeared on poster boards and T-shirts that she'd set up. Makoul got her to admit that she probably didn't hit the wood with as much force as the boys had used to hit the bodies, implying that the blood could have traveled farther than her experiment indicated. She also had not used the same type of weapon.

Dr. Mihalikis testified to the causes of death, stating again that there were three different weapons and therefore three different people involved. Since David had used the baseball bat, as he claimed in his statement, that left a pickax handle or metal bar for another perpetrator. The pickax handle bore blood from Erik and Brenda, and possibly from Dennis. While they already knew that David had been part of Dennis's murder, it was now clear that someone else was as well. Of Bryan and Benny, only Benny's shirt had spatters of Dennis's blood on it.

After a few more witnesses, the prosecution rested. Makoul told the press that Steinberg had presented a case of "total confusion" that had proven nothing. Now it was his turn. Makoul called a number of people who had heard Bryan and David make threats against their parents, but under cross-examination, some said that Benny might have been the leader of their little hate group. Then Makoul had psychologist Peter Badgio and psychiatrist Peter Bloom testify about Benny's mental state at the time of the crimes and directly afterward. Benny had developed acute stress disorder, they agreed, and rather than call the police, he'd fled with the brothers from fear that they would otherwise hurt him. The doctors also testified that IQ assessments affirmed his diagnosis of borderline mentally retarded.

Steinberg raised the issue that stress disorder tests must be performed shortly after the traumatic event, not a year later, so that made the results less than credible. Also, the prosecutor made certain the jury realized how silly one doctor's explanation was when he said that Benny's use of a false name for the hotel registry was a symptom of stress rather than an expedient way to disguise their trail.

Blood spatter pattern expert Neil Hoffman stated that the blood found on Benny's shirt could have been exhaled across the room by Dennis, or it could have traveled that far from the blows—about eight to eleven feet. He also testified that Dr. Barbara Rowley's blood splatter experiments were not reliable or replicable. Steinberg got Hoffman to admit, however, that he had not conducted his own experiments to prove this. (In other words, he hadn't done anything scientific to disprove her work or prove his own position.)

During the rebuttal of the mental illness testimony, a nurse at Lehigh County Prison testified that Benny was intelligent enough to have filled out a medical history sheet, and a school psychologist denied that he was mentally retarded. Dr. Robert Gordon, a clinical psychologist from the area and a renowned expert on the MMPI-2 personality assessment, said that Benny showed only normal signs of anxiety and, in fact, the test supported a diagnosis of a psychopathic personality. That meant Benny could probably deceive others with some skill, unhindered by guilt or remorse.

Then it was time to wrap things up. On April 25, 1996, during closing arguments, Makoul stressed that there was clearly reasonable doubt in this case. He re-emphasized Benny's low IQ and stress disorder. Steinberg argued that Benny had been a willing accomplice in three murders, but even if they believed it was only one, he was still a murderer. They sent this to the jury members, who listened to the judge's instructions and then retired to deliberate. The following day, they were ready with a verdict.

Benny Birdwell was found guilty of the first-degree murder of Dennis Freeman, but was found not guilty in the murders of Brenda and Erik. He was sentenced to life in prison without the possibility of parole. In the end, no one was convicted of killing Erik. Despite a series of appeals, including one in which Bryan wanted to act as his own attorney and contest his "coerced confession," as of this writing, all remain in prison.

But there was a ripple effect from all the publicity about this gruesome crime. Not far away in Lower Macungie, another young man was taking it all in and making his own plan.

Copy Cat

The Freeman family massacre had captivated sixteen-year-old Jeffrey Howorth. He'd watched every news show about the brothers' crime and capture, calling them "dumb" for getting caught. Yet, oddly, he had no affinity for their racist ideas or their method of aggression. He even deplored racism. Howorth was considered a good boy—shy and good-natured—who had never been in trouble. A member of the swim team at Emmaus High School, he was an average student. But he clearly had a dark side that few people saw—especially those most in danger. His mother had recently limited the hours she spent on the job because she sensed her youngest son was having a difficult time. Tragically, she was right, but she never saw what was coming.

The Howorths lived about ten miles from where the Freeman boys had killed their parents and brother. For some reason Jeffrey, too, wished to kill his parents. He had said as much to his older brother, Steven, home during that period from Penn State. What the Freeman brothers had done had apparently affirmed his desire and encouraged him to act. On the afternoon of March 2, 1995, he loaded a .22 caliber rifle and listened as his father came home around 5:00 P.M. and parked in the garage. Jeffrey waited in the kitchen and watched his father open the door. As George Howorth, 46, came in, Jeffrey shot him at point-blank range in the stomach. He then shot him four more times. One bullet hit George in the face and three others were to the front of his head. The man lay where he fell, still wearing his overcoat and gloves.

Fifteen minutes later, Jeffrey's mother, Susan, came home. She entered the kitchen and saw her husband lying prone and bleeding on the floor. As she dropped her purse in shock, Jeffrey exploited the opportunity to shoot her in the face. Yet she did not fall down and die. Instead, she managed to absorb the impact and run. She made it to the garage door, but he caught up to her and grabbed her coat. Pulling her back into the dining room while she screamed for him to let her go, he shot her again and finished her off. According to the pathology report completed by Lehigh Valley Hospital pathologist Sarah Funke, Susan was shot nine times, three in the front and six in the back.

Jeffrey seemed to have no feeling for what he'd done. He calmly washed his hands in the sink and then put ammunition, a .22-caliber rifle, a 12-gauge shotgun and some camping equipment into his mother's Chevy Lumina. He knew his brother, Steve, would be coming home soon and he wanted to be gone. In fact it was only minutes after he left that Steve arrived and discovered the prone bodies. He walked through the house to find Jeffrey and instead discovered a scribbled note on a desk in his room: "I told you I would do it, Steve. You can't say I didn't warn you." Stunned, he called the police.

An all-points bulletin was issued to try to apprehend the boy, but he had a head start. Jeffrey had gotten into the family's car and driven for two days until he ran out of gas, landing off Highway 70 in Callaway County, Missouri, just over an hour west of St. Louis. He had two dollars left. He left the car and went into the woods nearby, but when the police approached the car, he emerged and turned himself in. They returned him to Allentown. When asked how he was, he said simply, "I am bitter."

Items in the home that indicated Jeffrey's state of mind that day included jottings about his frustration with school, his anger over his parents' desire that he attend college, and ideas about murder. One note revealed his affinity with the Freemans. "Those kids in Salisbury Township were cool... They killed their parents." He'd expressed hope that a movie would be made about what he had done.

Howorth's trial started in July, 1995. Defense attorney Dennis Charles decided on an insanity defense, believing that something had caused Jeffrey to snap. But such a defense had worked only once before in that county. The prosecution team, headed by Assistant DA Douglas Reichley, used the notes left at the murder scene to argue that Jeffrey was just looking for attention. His true heart, they said, was darker than people had realized, proven by his excitement over the Freeman brothers' crimes. However, the jurors thought Jeffrey looked like a troubled youth, emotionally immobilized by his situation.

Dr. Timothy Michals, a psychiatrist, interviewed Howorth and learned that thoughts about parricide had first occurred to him at the age of five—around the same time he'd been diagnosed with a brain disorder that caused learning disabilities. He had expected to wait until he was thirty and then use a knife or some other sharp implement to hack both his mother and father to death. He had been inspired by the Freemans, he admitted, but had no allegiance to skinheads or neo-Nazis. His father had been a Boy Scout leader and Sunday school teacher, not a cruel or abusive parent. His mother had been a homemaker and reportedly a loving mother. The crime made little sense, apart from Jeffrey having an untreated mental illness that hindered his appreciation that what he had done was wrong.

The attorney played up the manic nature of Jeffrey's condition. He had overreacted to comments only days before when his gums had bled from brushing his teeth, and had threatened to kill his brother. He'd also suffered some academic setbacks, having received a low SAT score, failed a Spanish test and received Fs in other classes. He believed, said the attorney, that his parents would be severely disappointed over his failures, although he could offer no behavior on their part to substantiate this. He also showed no remorse for his crimes, which made the defense difficult.

Judge William Ford instructed the jury about the requirements for a finding of not guilty by reason of insanity, and they took four days to come up with that verdict. When he heard it, Howorth smiled. He was sent to the Norristown State Hospital for evaluation.

Each year since then, Howorth has been re-evaluated to determine if he can be freed, but as of this writing, he remains in the high-security Norristown hospital. In 2004, Judge Ford indicated that "Howorth continues to suffer from severe mental illness." His psychiatrist at Norristown stated that Howorth has made little progress in understanding the nature of his crime or what he must do to be released. "It's like there's a vacuousness there," she said, "an emotional shell." A therapist who worked with him told reporters that Howorth suffers from "stunted growth" in his cognitive processing skills, especially at emotional levels. He'd been given some responsibilities, which he performed well, but he continued to enjoy violent movies and to fail to understand what he did. He received medications, group therapy, and intensive counseling in anger management skills, with the hope that one day he could be returned to society. Early in 2008, he was re-committed for another year, although he'd shown progress and had been moved to a less restrictive unit.

Kindness Poorly Repaid

Also in Salisbury Township, not far from where the Freemans had lived, Samuel F. Hill was murdered and rolled into a tent to be unceremoniously dumped. It was but a short jaunt from his house to a once-pretty wooded park along Constitution Drive, where many people now illegally leave household trash, old tires, and even the rotting carcasses of de-antlered deer. (In fact, another human body would be dumped here only a few years later.) Samuel F. Hill had offered to help out his step-nephew, Alan Dale Borger, just released from state prison after serving time for burglary. Borger had lived in the modest home in Fountain Hill Heights only eleven days when he made his move.

Constitution Drive

A friend of Hill's saw him on October 14, 1990, but then he seemed to just disappear. His body was found six days later, inside a tent beneath a sheet, blanket and some pillows. He'd been bludgeoned to death. The bedding was also bloody. The friend knew that Hill used these items whenever he slept on the couch.

Borger was arrested, but he claimed he was innocent and stated that Hill's estranged wife's boyfriend might have killed Hill. However, there was incriminating evidence against Borger, including his inconsistent statements about when he had last seen Hill and the fact that he was in possession of valuable items belonging to Hill. Once police identified the body, Hill's friend went to his house and noticed that the sofa was wet and the living room unusually clean. The bedding that Hill always left on the sofa was gone, as were the sofa seat covers. Borger claimed he was washing these items. This was clearly a lie, as they never turned up. FBI lab tests revealed blood on areas of the couch where someone had attempted to clean it. A step-brother admitted to police that he'd seen Hill's watch, ring, and coin collection in Borger's possession a day after Hill had been killed. The defense used Borger's notion that someone else had killed Hill, but that didn't fly with the jury.

Street Where Hill Murder Took Place

Convicted of first-degree murder, Borger received a sentence of life in prison, but within three months he'd escaped with another inmate. He hung out in Easton and Salisbury Township for a while before he was finally apprehended and returned to prison.

While these crimes are shocking, a man in the northeastern part of Pennsylvania, had also committed murder, but with a higher victim toll.

Familicide

George Banks, a prison guard dressed in army fatigues and carrying a semi-automatic AR-15 rifle, began eliminating his family around 2:00 A.M. on September 25, 1982, in Wilkes-Barre, Pennsylvania. This is about an hour north of the Allentown area, but because it was so sensational, it's close enough for our purposes. Two step-children, who hid when they heard him, witnessed the horror as Banks broke into their trailer and killed their mother, grandmother, sister and half-brother. That same night Banks killed nine others, including a man just standing outside the home where the slaughter took place. He also shot another bystander, who survived.

Arrested and arraigned, Banks's attorney indicated that his client was mentally incompetent to stand trial because he'd been unaware of what he was doing. At the time of the shooting, Banks was on leave from his job because he had threatened to commit suicide and had expressed paranoid ideation about poison in his food. He felt suffocated.

Dr. Michael J. Spodak, Chief of Psychiatry at Baltimore County General Hospital in Maryland, examined Banks for his competence to stand trial and found him remorseful, but preoccupied with fears of a conspiracy. "He said he thinks someone moved the bodies around," Spodak commented, "and put extra bullets into them and changed some of the clothes." He diagnosed Banks as "terminally paranoid" and incompetent to stand trial.

However, Dr. Robert Sadoff examined Banks for the prosecution and said that while the accused had acted in a strange manner, he did understand the criminal nature of what he'd done. The judge declared Banks competent and the trial was on, centered largely on Banks's state of mind. The jury heard how he was the child of a black father and white mother, and although he had once married a black woman, at the time of the crime he had lived with three white women in a rundown house. In all, he had killed four women with whom he'd had children, seven children (five were his), an elderly woman, and a complete stranger. Associates indicated that he hated both races whose heritage he shared and felt relentlessly persecuted. He'd been in a dispute over child custody with the woman in the trailer home and had a history of battering.

Despite testimony about Banks's paranoia, his bizarre statements and his alleged motive of sparing his children from the racial biases he'd suffered, the jury convicted him of twelve counts of first-degree murder and sentenced him to death. In 2001, his death sentence was overturned on a technicality and in 2004 his case went to the state Supreme Court. A competency hearing was held in 2006 which ended with a ruling that Banks was too mentally ill to be executed. The state Supreme Court overturned the decision, ruling that a psychiatric expert for the prosecution had been precluded from testifying. Banks's

George Banks

attorneys have asked the court to reconsider. Banks, 65 at this writing, remains in prison.

While the slaughter of lovers and relatives is horrific, the motives are generally quite human and easy to grasp. Not so with our next category: the serial killers.

PART III: THE SERIAL KILLERS

The Lehigh Valley has seen two serial killers operating within its boundaries, and a third was living here at the time he was killing in a neighboring county. No area is immune from such people and there may be past killers we have yet to identify.

Heart of Stone

Somerset Medical Center in Somerville, New Jersey, was the facility that finally stopped a healthcare serial killer who had first cut a swath through Pennsylvania. On the night shift of June 15, 2003, a nurse submitted a computer order for the heart medication digoxin for a patient, although it had not been prescribed. Then the order was canceled, but the drug disappeared from the stock. Around the same time, someone accessed the records of Jin Kyung Han, a forty-year-old cancer patient. The following morning she went into a cardiac seizure. Her doctor was surprised to find a high level of digoxin in her system. He stabilized Han and ordered the nurses to be more careful.

Less than two weeks later, a sixty-eight-year-old Roman Catholic priest, Reverend Florian Gall, died. High levels of digoxin were found in his system as well, but since he was a heart patient this was not unexpected. It was just the wrong dose. Still, these cases raised a red flag.

The hospital administration sent the records and samples to the New Jersey poison control center and initiated an internal investigation. The state-of-the-art computerized care system at SMC, Cerner, allowed nurses to check patients' medical histories. Another system tracked all drugs used and opened a drawer to give workers access. Officials found that on the nights prior to both patients going into critical condition, a male nurse, Charles Cullen, had ordered digoxin for patients under his care. He had then canceled the orders. Yet the drug was clearly missing. They looked at his recommendations from prior employment, but there were no reports that signaled a red flag. In fact, he had often received glowing reviews from other hospitals where he'd worked.

Over the next few months, other patients suffered from having high levels of drugs in their systems, and Steven Marcus, a toxicologist and executive director of New Jersey Poison Information and Education System, warned SMC that they had an active poisoner on their staff. Administrators continued to monitor the situation throughout the fall of 2003, although they already knew that Cullen was a common factor.

When two more patients suffered similar overdoses, Cullen was fired. Somerset County Prosecutor Wayne Forrest initiated his own investigation and found that

Cullen had worked at an alarming number of health-care organizations. Notably, he'd been fired from several.

Charles Cullen

On December 12, 2003, Cullen was arrested as he left a restaurant and soon charged with the murder of Reverend Florian Gall and the attempted murder of Jin Kyung Han. With both cases, Cullen was suspected of injecting a lethal dose of digoxin, which he had procured via deceptive computer manipulation from hospital supplies. But he'd been ignorant about computer tracking: canceling the order failed to delete the transaction.

Cullen did not resist arrest. In court at his arraignment, he pled guilty to the charges and said he had no intention of fighting. "I don't intend to contest the charges," he uttered in a quiet voice. "I plan to plead guilty."

The judge asked him not to enter a plea at that time. Cullen's response was to rescind his request for a public defender. His bail was set at $1 million and he was taken to a jail in Somerset County.

But he had already dropped a bombshell on detectives a few days earlier during a seven-hour interrogation that went well beyond the current charges and would open up the largest murder investigation in that county's history. To Detectives Timothy Braun and Daniel Baldwin, Cullen described how easy it had been to go from one facility to the next as he killed patients, moving on as soon as suspicions were voiced. He said that some of his bosses had known the errors he'd made that harmed patients, but they'd overlooked them.

Cullen claimed that he had killed patients to end their suffering, which seemed viable, since he'd often been around critical-care and burn-ward patients. He had also put insulin into IV bags stored in a closet, apparently just to see what would happen. Clearly this malicious mischief had nothing to do with mercy. Cullen also said he'd wanted to quit, but had bills to pay and children to support. Yet he made no mention of attempting to look for another line of work. Even his counselor thought he should stop nursing, he said, because he wasn't dealing with his depression very well. He felt he had no choice, but to keep doing what he was doing.

He mentioned that he thought that patients were being treated as nonhumans, and that was so difficult for him to watch that he decided to end their suffering. "I couldn't stop myself," he said. "I just couldn't stop."

More charges followed. Over sixteen years, in ten different institutions, Cullen admitted he'd intentionally overdosed thirty, possibly forty patients. He didn't have an exact count, but he was clearly a serial killer of major proportions.

Cullen expected to get the death penalty, but less than a week after his explosive arraignment, he accepted public defender Johnnie Mask, who subsequently said Cullen might offer names in exchange for taking the death penalty off the table. Both Pennsylvania and New Jersey had to agree to the terms. Detectives were already busy putting his record together and contacting institutions in Pennsylvania, such as Lehigh Valley Hospital in Allentown and St. Luke's in Bethlehem, to ask what they knew about their former employee. But getting the goods on him without his cooperation was going to be difficult.

Zachary Lysek heard about the investigation and remembered what had happened in 1999. Suspecting an "angel of death" at Easton Hospital, he'd examined the death circumstances of a 78-year-old patient, Ottomar Schramm, and thought he might have been murdered. Schramm had succumbed to a fatal dose of digoxin, although his condition had not warranted getting this drug. While Lysek could not prove where Schramm had received the medication, since he'd come to the hospital from a nursing home, he was certain that someone had administered it with evil intent. He requested an internal investigation at the hospital, based on reports from one of Schramm's relatives about who had been near the patient, but it proved inconclusive. Lysek was frustrated. He *knew* that something was amiss. But Cullen had already moved on to St. Luke's in Fountain Hill.

Then in 2002, Lysek heard from a nurse at St. Luke's about suspicious behavior by one of her fellow nurses, Charles Cullen. Lysek had contacted the Lehigh County DA. A nurse had investigated on her own and in June 2002, she had found opened and unopened packages of drugs improperly placed in a bin. She'd also seen Cullen leaving the rooms of patients who then expired.

Hospital Where Cullen Worked

When Cullen was pressured about this, he resigned and moved on. The state hired Dr. Isadore Mihalakis to make a comprehensive investigation, but in March 2003, he issued a report indicating that, after reviewing 67 cases, he had no proof of criminal activity. The hospital administrators notified the Pennsylvania Board of Nursing about Cullen's unprofessional conduct, but without better proof that was all they could do.

Thus, on behalf of families who wanted closure, officials from both states agreed to Cullen's terms. As the cases were opened and people were named, it would become clear that a number of the victims had not been suffering and some were even on the mend. Cullen had offered reasons for killing that did not add up, but the fact that he was having trouble in nearly every area of his life during the time he was ending the lives of patients, indicates a possibility that he was taking out his sense of failure on them.

Cullen was the youngest of nine brothers and sisters who grew up in West Orange, New Jersey. Their father was a bus driver, their mother a home-maker. Born in 1960, Cullen lived in a working-class neighborhood. His father died when he was seven months old and later, when he was in high school, his mother was in a fatal car accident. Two of his siblings had also died young, and he cared for one of them during the process.

In 1978, Cullen dropped out of high school and enlisted in the Navy, serving on a nuclear submarine. When he was discharged in 1984, he attended the Mountainside Hospital School of Nursing. By 1988, he had his first job as a nurse. He soon got married and had two daughters, but that did not last. Cullen's wife had filed for a restraining order against him, based on her fear that he might endanger her and their two children. In court papers, she indicated that he had spiked people's drinks with lighter fluid, burned his daughters' books, and showed extreme cruelty to the family pets.

He apparently racked up a number of moving violations during this time as well, and he was steadily deteriorating in other ways. On January 22, 1993, Cullen received the divorce papers, and a few weeks later he was arrested for stalking another nurse. Apparently, after they'd gone out once, he offered her an engagement ring and she turned him down. He then broke into her home, ostensibly "concerned" about her, but more likely to show her how vulnerable she was. For this incident, he drew a year's probation. At this time, Cullen admitted himself into a psychiatric facility. On two occasions that same year, he was accused of domestic violence, and he tried to kill himself.

All of this was going on when he killed three elderly female patients in New Jersey. Just days after his wife sent inspectors to Cullen's apartment to examine it for fire hazards, Cullen killed 90-year-old Lucy Mugavero. In June, he agreed to submit to a polygraph (and passed) to show that he had not neglected his children or abused alcohol in their presence. In July, he killed 85-year-old Mary Natoli. In August, a caseworker reported that Cullen had not addressed his alcohol addiction, so he recommended that all visits with the children be supervised. Within weeks, Cullen killed Helen Dean. The record for this one-year period clearly shows that when things went wrong, Cullen reacted with aggression toward those who could not protect themselves.

In 1997, he was taken to a hospital in New Jersey for depression. He refused to provide a blood sample and afterward filed a police report against the doctor. Just over two years later, he made a suicide attempt, but was saved by a neighbor. In 1998, he filed for bankruptcy and had a pile of debts and back payments due in child support to the tune of over $66,000. He lost his dog to the animal protection agency. Yet many colleagues recalled him as a gentle person willing to put in extra hours. He was always ready to medicate people in pain.

As the case against him progressed, Cullen was transferred to the Anne Klein Forensic Center in Trenton, New Jersey, where a panel of professionals examined him. He surrendered his New Jersey and Pennsylvania nursing licenses. Every hospital that had ever employed Cullen looked over its records and re-examined its procedures. Nurses at St. Luke's told reporters that by their count, Cullen had worked just over 20% of the total hours available in critical care, but was present for over 56% of the deaths.

But Cullen was full of surprises. In June 2005, local newspapers published the results of a long meeting with Cullen in which he offered advice for healthcare institutions on how to make it more difficult for people like him to do what he did. One of his MOs had been to get medications by opening patients' drawers, because no one tracked the drugs. When electronic drug tracking was put into place, he simply learned how to manipulate computers. There was no system in place for making people who got the drugs accountable for them. In another place, he recalled a storage room for drugs was never locked and it was easy for him to pilfer them. He claimed he threw away thousands of dollars worth of pharmaceuticals, but no one seemed to notice.

There should be protocols for accountability for staff and for drug-handling procedures, he advised. Among them would be installing surveillance cameras, the use of swipe cards and bar codes, and a daily count of lethal medications. He also said there should be a national database for updating employment history of healthcare workers. Institutions should pass information along to one another, Cullen advised, and hospitals should pay attention to the mental health of their employees. Poor performance such as his should be reported to the state board of nursing.

Cullen went to court in New Jersey on March 2, 2006, to receive eleven life sentences, while about twenty relatives of his victims battered him with insults. Then, on March 10, he went to Allentown, Pennsylvania, where he made a scene. Judge William Platt had made a public comment that Cullen did not like, so he began the proceedings by saying, "Your honor, you need to step down."

Judge Platt said he intended to preside over the hearing. Cullen continued to insist he step down with a repetitive chant, "Your honor, you need to step down." Platt ordered that Cullen be gagged, so a cloth was placed over his face with a mesh hood to hold it over his mouth, but he chanted in a muffled manner. Victims' relatives were frustrated in their attempts to be heard. At the close of this hearing, he received seven more life sentences.

Cullen went to the New Jersey State Prison in Trenton to serve his eighteen consecutive life sentences and his attorney hired several psychologists to do a formal assessment. A psychologist from Allentown told reporters at the *Morning Call* that Cullen had identified with the pain of his patients and had killed them as a way to relieve his own pain and depression.

People with experience in the psychology of healthcare serial killers would hesitate to accept statements from such killers at face value. Most of them initially claim motives of mercy and yet their actual behavior undermines that. It appeared more likely that, similar to others in his position, Cullen had killed because he derived something from it that satisfied him. Not all of the patients were dying or in pain. Some were recovering or were in no danger at all.

Late in April 2004, Cullen pled guilty to murdering thirteen patients in New Jersey, one in Pennsylvania, and to the attempted murder of two more patients in his care. His last murder took place just ten days before he was fired—while he was under investigation by several agencies.

Officials in both states went to work on new policies and procedures for health-care facilities. State regulators in New Jersey strengthened nursing standards, with new rules and harsher penalties. They also introduced the Safe Health Care Reporting Act, which would expand the current National Practitioner Data Bank to include all licensed healthcare workers, not just physicians. Legislation was considered in both Pennsylvania and New Jersey to protect hospitals from lawsuits should they have reason to offer a negative evaluation to a former employee's new employer. In April 2004, New Jersey's governor signed a law that requires all healthcare facilities in the state to document and report serious medical errors, and some Pennsylvania hospitals will tell prospective employees that they will pass along whatever negative information they acquire.

As of this writing, Cullen has admitted to 29 murders and six attempted murders, without apology. According to his deal, he is still required to assist in other investigations, so there may be future revelations. In January 2008, the *Morning Call* reported that Cullen's cooperative tone had disappeared. Attorneys are seeking his help in their civil lawsuits, but with no death penalty hanging over his head, the state has lost its leverage.

Harvey

On the morning of June 9, 1993, the police investigated a suspicious incident in Allentown, Pennsylvania. A woman on East Gordon Street had looked out her window and seen a newspaper cart abandoned between two parked cars. She knew it was uncharacteristic of the fifteen-year-old carrier, Charlotte Schmoyer, to be negligent, so she phoned the police. Schmoyer's supervisor had not heard from her and could not locate her. The police found the girl's bicycle abandoned as well, along with her portable radio. She was not at home, only blocks away, and the situation now looked grim. A neighbor reported a light blue car in the area that morning.

A few hours later, DA Robert Steinberg accompanied the police as they followed a tip about a light blue car to a wooded area at the East Side Reservoir. A trail of blood led from the parking lot and they found a discarded shoe. Then the girl's body turned up in the woods, covered with dead leaves and heavy logs.

The autopsy revealed that Schmoyer had been raped and stabbed twenty-two times in the back and neck before her throat was slashed. Three superficial cuts indicated that a knife had been held to her throat during her ordeal. A pubic hair was found on Schmoyer's navy sweatshirt and a head hair on her knee. This could help to identify her killer. There were no real leads, so this shocking crime went unsolved for the moment. The FBI, with an office in Allentown, offered the services of its Behavioral Sciences Unit. No one realized at the time that they may have a serial killer in the area.

Schmoyer, it later turned out, was actually the second victim, grabbed near where the first one had been stalked and attacked the year before. Twenty-nine-year-old Mary Burghardt had reported that someone had cut through a screen door and entered her apartment. She assured her parents she would be more careful about locking her doors, yet two days later, on August 9, 1992, a man tore through the front window screen and came at her, smacking her hard in the head. She managed to pound on the wall and scream for help, but he bludgeoned her with a blunt weapon until she fell to the floor. The autopsy revealed that he had delivered some thirty-seven blows to her head.

Now that he'd killed twice, apparently enjoying it, he started to stalk a third victim, a story that became highly publicized later in national magazines (the only reason we name her). Denise Sam-Cali, 37, lived on the East Side of Allentown. She usually walked a mile each morning to the limousine and bus service she owned with her husband, John. They went away for a few days, returning on June 17. To their shock, they found the back door of their home slightly open. John went inside to look around, but saw no immediate evidence of a burglary. Nevertheless, someone had clearly been there, as a bottle had been moved and they found a dirty footprint on the couch. John soon discovered that his gun collection was missing.

The knowledge that someone not only had those guns, but had entered their home, left the Sam-Calis with pervasive feelings of fear. John purchased more guns for self-protection and Denise learned to shoot. Soon another incident occurred not far away.

On June 20, the predator entered the home of a woman he'd been watching. However, he found her in bed upstairs with her boyfriend. Apparently he decided not to risk confronting a male, but he looked around on the second floor and spotted the woman's five-year-old daughter asleep. He choked her into unconsciousness and carried her, by the neck, downstairs. She revived and tried to scream, but he dumped her headfirst into a laundry basket of towels and dirty clothes and raped her. Then he choked her again and she passed out.

Early the following morning, the girl woke her mother to tell her what had happened, so the woman's boyfriend checked downstairs and found a screen from a window removed. The victim's mother saw small hemorrhages in the child's eyes and bruises that indicated she had been choked and hit. She took the girl to a doctor, who found that she had been sexually attacked.

Allentown residents were understandably alarmed. More people locked their doors and windows, but that did not stop the marauder. A month later, he struck again. Denise Sam-Cali was home alone on June 28. John was on a business trip, but due back soon. She had come in late after visiting her aunt down the street, so she was ready to go right to bed. She undressed and crawled under the sheets.

Suddenly she caught her breath. She was sure she'd heard something inside the house, like crackling paper.

"Who's there?" she shouted.

But the place was silent.

Deciding she'd be safer with a neighbor, Denise jumped out of bed, grabbed a comforter to cover herself, and ran down the hall. To her horror, a man emerged from a walk-in closet with a knife in his hand. Denise raced for the door, but he got there first and grabbed her arm. He tried to stab her in the face, managing to cut her lip. She knocked the knife away and struggled to get out. He still had a firm grip on her arm, but she broke free and got outside.

On the lawn, the man caught her by the hair and threw her to the ground. She tried to scream, but no sound came from her. As he assaulted her he strangled her. Denise bit her attacker and cried out. He hit her in the face and choked her until she lost consciousness.

A neighbor who heard the commotion turned on an outside floodlight, which frightened the attacker off. Denise regained consciousness and managed to crawl back into her house to call 9-1-1. The police arrived and took her to the hospital, where nurses processed her with a rape kit. They attended to her bruised face and the bruises on her neck. She was aware how lucky she was to be alive. The police soon found a knife the intruder had grabbed in the Sam-Cali's kitchen; it was wrapped in a napkin and left on the floor of their home.

As well as she could, Denise gave the police a description of her attacker: his eyes had been intense with rage and desperation... and they had seemed evil. He'd been white, about five-foot-seven, muscular, young, and clean-shaven.

The Sam-Calis installed a burglar alarm system, but to their consternation the intruder managed to break in again. One day, the new Colt .380 automatic handgun, left on a table, turned up missing. The DA believed this rapist would certainly revisit the home to silence the witness and wondered if he could work this to an advantage. He asked John and Denise to remain in the home, seemingly vulnerable, but under police protection, to lure him back. They bravely accepted.

Officer Brian Lewis stayed in the home night after night for a couple of weeks to watch for the intruder's return. However, the offender had already moved his hunting ground a mile away as he looked for his fifth victim.

53

He'd spotted another large-boned white woman, and he'd followed her until he saw where she lived. Jessica Jean Fortney, 47, lived with her grown daughter, son-in-law, and their seven-year-old child. On July 14, these three were asleep on the second floor, with loud fans on, when the man came in and attacked Fortney in the living room, breaking her nose with a weapon. Then he raped and strangled her, leaving her blood-covered body on the sofa beneath a blanket.

Fortney's grandchild had seen the assault from her bedroom. Her description matched Denise Sam-Cali's. Officials realized they had a dangerous serial rapist-killer at large who was striking quickly and often. Without clues, they had to look at the crimes, and there were important similarities among at least four of them. They had all been committed in the same general area, three of the victims were large buxom women, and except for Charlotte, they were all attacked inside their homes after the offender had entered through a window.

The police could only hope the killer would make a mistake and try yet again to kill the one woman who had survived. Their fear was that he would begin to roam a larger area, as his latest crime suggested. But then they got a break.

Two weeks had passed, and each night officers stayed inside the Cali home. No one knew if this plan would pay off, but they continued to watch. Around 1:30 A.M. on July 31, Officer Lewis heard a distinctive noise: Someone was prying at the patio door. A few moments later, the front door handle jiggled. This was it: Someone was trying to get in. Lewis knew that some of the windows were open to make it easy to enter, and they were near lamps left burning, so he waited.

A hand reached in through the living room window, wearing a black glove, and deftly removed the screen. Lewis crouched, ready to shoot. He pressed a button on a radio handset through which he could notify his back-up without giving himself away.

The window was quietly eased open and a thick-bodied man dressed in black shoved himself over the frame and into the room. He was young and short, just as Sam-Cali had described, and he was quick.

"Halt!" Lewis shouted as he rose to show himself. "Police!"

Though taken by surprise, the intruder sprinted past Lewis toward the dark kitchen and reached for a gun on his waistband. Lewis shot at him, but he kept running and returned the gunfire, forcing Lewis to take cover and shoot again. Lewis then stepped out and shot several times toward the kitchen. He missed and the intruder managed to shoot at him again.

Because he needed to reload, Lewis went to the bedroom to reassure the couple, and they could all hear the intruder banging on the dead-bolted back door and kitchen walls, trying to get out. Lewis instructed the Sam-Calis to stay out of the way as he prepared to face the desperate gunman. He was aware that back-up had arrived and knew they would be circling the house, but suddenly the place went quiet.

Lewis edged cautiously toward the kitchen, uncertain what to expect and keeping his freshly-loaded gun drawn. As he drew closer, he anticipated that the intruder might spring out at him or fire from some dark area. Lewis neared the door to the kitchen. Tense, his heart pounding, he still heard nothing. Then he saw several broken windows on the wooden door. The man had managed to force his way out and slip away, although he'd left a lot of blood behind on the door.

Calls were made to area hospitals to watch for anyone with a bad cut or a bullet wound. It was just a matter of time, they now believed, perhaps only minutes.

Around 5:30 A.M., a young man showed up at the Lehigh Valley Hospital ER to get his cuts treated. His arm and leg were bleeding badly. Before he was treated, he started to leave, but was quickly detained. Lewis arrived to identify him as the person who'd shot at him hours earlier. His name was Harvey Miguel "Miggy" Robinson and he lived in the East Side vicinity with his mother. He was only eighteen and he insisted he was innocent. The evidence would indicate otherwise. Robinson was booked and arraigned on multiple charges, including breaking and entering, burglary, aggravated assault and attempted homicide, and held in lieu of $1 million bail. Denise Sam-Cali testified at his hearing that she could identify Robinson as the man who attacked her and she fully described her ordeal. Other evidence against him included Officer Lewis's identification, a bite mark that Sam-Cali claimed to have given Robinson during her assault, black gloves found in Robinson's bedroom, as well as the .380 handgun stolen from the Calis and casings that matched those from bullets fired in their home.

Harvey Robinson

The police also searched two cars, a light blue Ford Tempo GL belonging to Robinson's mother, which was similar to the car seen in the neighborhood when Charlotte Schmoyer was abducted, and Robinson's gray Dodge Laser SE. His blood was in both.

For his arraignment, Robinson wore a bulletproof vest. Police had learned that between the Burghardt and Schmoyer murders, he'd been institutionalized for burglary, but had no history of mental illness. Investigators believed that he had either known his victims or had stalked them before raping or killing them. He may have burglarized Burghardt's apartment a few days before he killed her.

In December 1993, just after Robinson turned 19, the papers announced that DNA tests from his blood samples linked him via semen to the three rape/murders and the two rapes. His blood and hair were found on Schmoyer, and both the little girl who survived and Denise Sam-Cali identified him as their attacker. Investigators did not believe he was responsible for any other murders in the area, but Special Agent Dennis Buckley of the FBI's Allentown office said that he fit the behavior of a serial killer, according to the Bureau's definition. Three victims in three separate instances with a cooling off period was the norm, and Robinson had likely intended to kill the two survivors. He had also used the same *modus operandi*, breaking into a home, choking and bludgeoning the victim, raping her, and leaving her dead or nearly dead.

DA Robert Steinberg led the prosecution while Robinson's family had hired David Nicholls to defend him. Nicholls immediately questioned the validity of the DNA evidence. It was a common ploy for defense attorneys in those days, because while DNA analysis had been confirmed as a viable science by this time (with the first U. S. conviction in 1987), attorneys had gained some ground by questioning laboratory corruption and poor handling of evidence. Nicholls suggested that there were problems with the subjectivity of the technicians, as well as the exposure of the biological samples to the environment, and even mentioned the possible fallibility of the test itself.

Supervisory Special Agent Harold Deadman, with the FBI lab, put the specimens through testing, along with specimens from other men in the area with a history of sex crimes, but only Robinson was a match to the samples from the victims. The state police lab confirmed this with its own tests. While the prosecution viewed its case as secure, they knew that DNA testimony was tricky. The first case to be decided involved the assault of Denise Sam-Cali.

DA Steinberg told Denise that Robinson would plead guilty in return for a reduced sentence and no trial. She initially declined it, but at an April 13 hearing, she accepted. Semen samples removed from her shortly after she was attacked were matched via DNA analysis to Robinson, and she identified him as her attacker. In addition, he had a gun in his possession stolen from the house, and Officer Lewis testified that Robinson was the man with whom he'd had a shoot-out.

Robinson said nothing during the hearing and his attorney called no one to speak on his behalf. Nicholls made it clear that the defendant had long been a troubled young man with a difficult life. Still, he offered no motive for Robinson's attacks, but he did describe the young man's good qualities: a high IQ that allowed him to get his high school equivalency diploma when he was sixteen and a good relationship with a loving mother.

Steinberg told reporters afterward, "He is everything that is evil in society, all rolled up in one person." But Nicholls asked for leniency and suggested that Robinson could be rehabilitated. Yet Robinson had been resistant to rules and aggressive toward others since the first grade. He'd committed his first juvenile offense, a theft, at the age of nine. Each time he got out of juvenile detention, he committed more antisocial acts. His chances for rehabilitation seemed slim at best. He was sentenced to 40 to 80 years in state prison.

Robinson had been an impulsive child with little ability to focus, a great deal of moodiness and a hair-trigger temper. After his first arrest at age nine, over the next eight years, he piled up a dozen more arrests, mostly for theft and property crimes. He fought with authority figures, had a history of substance abuse, and had been diagnosed with conduct disorders that were precursors to an adult antisocial personality disorder. Robinson spent many years in and out of different juvenile facilities, and the family frequently changed its residence. Due in part to his undisciplined behavior, he was held back in the first grade. He once assaulted a male middle school teacher, assigned to watch emotionally disturbed youths, in the classroom.

Yet he did have good points. At Dieruff High School, he wrestled, participated in cross-country sports, and played soccer and football, receiving trophies for his skill and ability. He was also a good student, excelling academically and earning awards for his essays. Some teachers believed he showed promise, even though he would need a great deal of support and guidance. But awards and trophies, and even recommendations, are difficult to reconcile with the rash of multiple rapes and brutally violent murders.

Robinson received a public defender, Carmen Marinelli, for his next court appearance. Marinelli requested three separate trials, as well as a change of venue, due to the amount of publicity the case had generated in the Lehigh Valley. Steinberg hoped for a single trial, and he demonstrated the strong similarities in the three cases, with DNA links to Robinson. He called FBI analyst Stephen Etter to explain the indicators known to experts that the murders were the work of a sexually-motivated serial killer. The judge decided to hold a single trial in Allentown, appointing James Burke to join the defense.

The prosecution lined up fifty witnesses to prove Robinson's participation in all three murders. Along with blood, hair, and semen evidence against Robinson, there had also been a sneaker impression on the face of one victim similar to sneakers that he'd worn. At this trial, Denise Sam-Cali was a witness. Robinson did not speak on his own behalf, despite his own attorneys' request to do so.

The proceeding lasted three weeks, and on November 8, 1994, Harvey Miguel Robinson was convicted of the rapes and murders of Burghardt, Schmoyer, and Fortney. During the sentencing phase, Robinson once again rejected his attorneys' plea to testify on his own behalf, so the jury heard from other witnesses about his difficult life.

"If there ever was a case where the death penalty was warranted," Steinberg was quoted as saying, "this is such a case." He offered four aggravating circumstances: multiple victims, murder committed during other felonies, torture of the victims (backed up by the pathologist's report from the condition of the bodies), and a history of violent aggression and threats. This was a man inherently dangerous to society, Steinberg insisted, and to emphasize this he showed nine graphic color photos of the bodies.

For the defense, Dr. Robert Sadoff, a forensic psychiatrist, testified that Robinson suffered from a dependency on drugs and alcohol and had an antisocial personality disorder. He'd also experienced visual and auditory hallucinations, and all of this had contributed to his difficulty in adjusting to social norms. Sadoff suggested that Robinson may have turned to rape and murder to relieve stress. However, he added, if these young offenders receive help in a controlled setting at an early age, they can improve. Under cross examination, he did concede that he would label a person who has killed three times in the manner of Robinson's offenses a serial killer.

Robinson's half-sister, cousin and a friend testified for him as well. They said that he was a good friend, but his disadvantage lay in having poor male role models, an alcoholic father and an older half-brother who were also criminals. The imprisoned half-brother, George Robbins, said that he and Robinson had converted to Islam and now believed in humility and peace. He begged for mercy.

Nevertheless, on November 10, the jury sentenced Robinson to die by lethal injection. Relatives of the victims broke down in tears, but Robinson himself showed no reaction; he retained the same blank expression he had worn throughout the trial.

Six months later, he was convicted of rape and the attempted murder of the five-year-old girl. Fifty-seven years were added to his sentences, and forty more for his July 31 shoot-out with the police.

On appeal, Robinson argued that his trial attorneys had failed to tell him the importance of testifying in his own behalf, hurting his chance for a fair trial, so he insisted he get an opportunity to redress the harm done. His new attorney, Philip Lauer, challenged Robinson's convictions on the grounds that there were fundamental flaws in the trial procedures. Among them was the fact that Sam-Cali's testimony had been admitted, although she had not recalled being sexually assaulted until after a detective had hypnotized her. And there were problems with that procedure: The hypnotist had learned details about the assault prior to putting Sam-Cali into a trance. There was a possibility that he had suggested details to her and she had incorporated them into her memory. There was research to show that such things occurred. In any event, Robinson's defense attorneys were not notified of this procedure and thus did not have the chance to test Sam-Cali's memory independently.

Other issues that Robinson raised involved a racially-biased jury selection (because they were selected based on having a driver's license), an error in allowing the three murders to be jointly tried, and an error in not changing the venue. Then on November 24, to the surprise of many, Robinson got his day in court.

Now 23, Robinson testified for three hours in front of about thirty people, denying he'd committed the slayings and indicating that he regretted not proclaiming his innocence to the jury members who had convicted him. At the time of his trial, he said, he'd given Marinelli and Burke the names of several people who could testify to his whereabouts when the three women were killed, as well as friends, coaches, teachers, and relatives who could attest to his good character. Yet they had called none of them. In addition, he continued, they did not inform him of the best strategy for defending himself and they did not use information about his childhood that might have helped him. He hoped to have his sentences vacated, have the charges dismissed altogether, or receive the opportunity for a new trial.

Robinson said he'd declined to testify during his trial because he worried that prosecutors could have questioned him about his guilty plea to raping Sam-Cali. "I was under the impression," he stated, "that if I did testify, then my past record was admissible." He said he'd not been informed otherwise. Prosecutor Jacqueline Paradis raised the issue that his life had been on the line and wondered how he had not understood the significance. He said he hadn't thought it was important.

Burke, one of Robinson's former defense attorneys, also testified, disputing his claim about the defense strategy. He insisted that he and Marinelli had repeatedly encouraged Robinson to testify. "I begged him," Burke stated. While he could not dispute the fact that only a few witnesses from Robinson's list had testified, he claimed that his and Marinelli's choices at the time had been made in their client's best interest: Many potential witnesses were contacted, he stated, but some seemed damaging to Robinson, while others refused to testify or could not be located.

The court deliberated over these revelations and decided that Robinson's attorneys had acted in his best interests and had not been ineffective in their counsel, so he did not receive a new trial.

In June 2001, Judge Edward Reibman vacated Robinson's death sentences in the murders of Burghardt and Schmoyer. In that trial, Reibman said, the instructions to the jury had improperly defined the aggravated circumstances of multiple murder. He allowed the defendant to have a new sentencing hearing.

Four years later, in December 2005, the Pennsylvania Supreme Court affirmed the death sentence in the Fortney case and the first-degree murder convictions in the other two cases. The high court stated that although Robinson believed his attorney had not presented mitigating circumstances, the trial jury had indeed considered reasons against imposing the death penalty and had given him death anyway. The court similarly rejected Robinson's claims that the prosecutor had improperly labeled him a predator. So Robinson remained in the same boat, until a development occurred on a national level.

On March 1, 2006, the U. S. Supreme Court ruled that juveniles age 17 and under were ineligible for the death penalty. This ruling affected Robinson's conviction in the Burghardt murder, committed when he was seventeen. However, that death sentence was already vacated. The Supreme Court's decision simply meant that Lehigh County District Attorney James Martin would not reopen that case, but he was determined to seek a new hearing in the Schmoyer case.

Robinson's death penalty appeal to the U.S. Supreme Court had been denied in October 2005. In February 2006, Pennsylvania Governor Ed Rendell signed his death warrant, with an execution date set for April 4, 2006. A federal appeal stayed it.

From prison, Robinson has posted comments on prisoner Web sites. He indicates that he enjoys exercise, writing, music, and reading self-help books. He particularly likes to help others. "Life is so truly precious," he writes, "so anything I can do for another is something I'm interested in and like."

Like the next predator we consider, Harvey seems to have little comprehension of the pain and suffering he inflicted on others.

Living Here, Killing There

The *Morning Call* printed a front-page story on April 20, 2008, about the confession of an Allentown-based serial killer, Timothy Krajcir, who had committed one of his admitted nine murders nearby (and the rest in three other states). He said the incident took place the week before Easter in 1979. It wasn't Krajcir's habit to enter a home spontaneously. While he selected victims at random—within certain manageable parameters—he generally checked out the residence to make sure he could get inside without much trouble and that the targeted victim appeared unprotected. Just north of Reading, in Muhlenberg Township of Berks County, he looked inside the modest home of fifty-one-year-old Myrtle Rupert, a registered nurse and head of pediatrics. He'd once lived in the area and was there visiting relatives. Recently caught molesting a girl in Illinois, and still awaiting a hearing on that charge, he'd already killed and raped other women.

Timothy Krajcir

The next day, Krajcir returned to the brick home, made sure the resident was away, and broke in. He cut the phone lines and then lay on her bed, waiting for her to return. However, when Rupp came home, she had company, so Krajcir exited without notice. He apparently knew or assumed she reported the break-in, because he came back a week later, posing with a fake badge as a police officer to "further investigate." Rupp was alone this time and she let him in. He took the opportunity to bind, rape and strangle her. The next day, on April 17, a neighbor was alerted by a paperboy to the open door, and when she entered she found Rupp's bound, nude body in the bedroom.

It was three decades later that Krajcir would face these charges in Berks County, thanks to a cold case review that relied on preserved evidence and a DNA analysis of the bedspread on which Rupp had been raped. Through closed-circuit television, Krajcir waived his right to a preliminary hearing and later pled guilty. "She didn't deserve to die," he stated. For this crime, he received a life sentence to tack on to those he is already serving at the maximum security Tamms Correctional Facility in Illinois. Krajcir apparently told a detective that he was going to come clean whenever his health failed, but the DNA analysis accelerated his confession. He also admitted to burglarizing numerous homes in Wescoesville and around Berks County.

Krajcir committed his first rape in 1963, a year after his stint in the Navy got him stationed in Illinois. The next sexual assault, four months later, involved a stabbing. He was soon under arrest for both incidents. He pled guilty and spent thirteen years in prison. Upon his release, he roved around, killing three women before being arrested for taking indecent liberties with a thirteen-year-old. Yet, he remained free on bail, and within a week he had raped another woman. Then he killed a woman in Kentucky before "visiting family" and ending Myrtle Rupp's life. At his hearing for the indecency charge, he accepted a designation of "sexually dangerous," getting more jail time, but within two years was free to rape, assault, and kill again (including a murder for which another man was convicted). In south Allentown in 1983, he assaulted three women before he was arrested.

Sent to Lehigh County prison, about five months later Krajcir decided to escape. He slipped off his rope made from bed sheets, fell onto a car, and broke his leg. He received a sentence of two-and-a-half to five years for the assaults. Since it was found that he'd violated parole in Illinois, in 1988 he was transferred back there. Two decades went by before he was charged with a murder. He pled guilty and received a forty-year sentence. In 2008, Krajcir pled guilty to five murders in Missouri and another in Illinois, as well as seven more sexual assaults. He received thirteen life sentences, but remained in maximum security in Illinois. When he made his confession in Missouri, he revealed his typical modus operandi.

Krajcir told reporters that he'd taken criminal justice courses, learning how crimes were investigated, which taught him how to commit crimes that left little evidence or an incriminating trail. Back then, no one knew how DNA analysis would revolutionize investigation, especially for sexual assaults, so he'd believed he was taking all precautions. Even so, Krajcir's success derived largely from luck, and in the end it was persistent investigators who brought him down.

Lt. Paul Echols, aware that DNA databases for convicted felons are regularly updated, resubmitted DNA evidence from the murder of a Missouri college student, Deborah Sheppard. He came up with a hit on Krajcir, in prison in Illinois for sexual offenses that got his DNA profile into the database. In another jurisdiction, detective Jim Smith did the same thing, linking Krajcir to several murders in Cape Girardieu. With the goods on him, prosecutors offered a deal: confess and avoid the death penalty. That way they could close the cases and possibly solve others.

Reportedly, Krajcir's killings were sexually driven, in which, as he put it, "all rationality is gone." Something supposedly "took him over" and transformed him into a different person. (It sounds like he's reading a script from Ted Bundy.) Ordinarily, he said, he likes people and even gets weepy over sentimental movies. "Believe it or not," he said, "I'm the type of person who likes to be liked." He told an interviewer how much he regretted his crimes and said he had a hard time understanding why he'd committed them. Yet their brutality belies this; he clearly targeted victims, terrorized them, and used them for his own purposes, without a thought for them or their loved ones. It's easy for him to cry now, but the typical psychopath is always ready with the "poor me" excuse.

An ambulance driver, Krajcir had the opportunity to scout out strategic places to sit and watch for victims. "I worked for the ambulance service saving lives," he stated, "and here I was taking them." His strategy was to sit in his car near parks, grocery stores, or shopping centers and watch for women alone. Then he'd follow them to see where they lived, watch this place for a while, and return later to break in while they were gone and wait for them. He liked neighborhoods that were not well-lighted. To prevent leaving fingerprints, he wore gloves, and he also tied a blue bandanna across his face. He had no particular victim type, he said, aside from female, and the women he killed at random ranged in age and appearance. Mostly, they were victims of opportunity. He would follow them to their homes, or see them there, and then break in through a door or window. (He described how he held his coat over a window and then used a rock to break it.) Often they screamed, but he'd continue with his plan, despite the possibility that someone may have heard it. After he stole a gun during a burglary, he used it as a murder weapon.

In 1977, Krajcir held a mother and daughter captive in Missouri; the father had called from the hospital and the daughter answered the phone and told him she loved him. Krajcir thought they did not realize that he might really kill them. But he was determined to leave no witnesses, so he slaughtered both. A few months later, he grabbed a young woman from a parking lot and forced her into his car, taking her home to rape, and then shooting her in the back of the head and dumping her body at a rest area. In 1982 in the same state, he strangled one woman and shot another, both inside their homes. He also broke into a home and raped three women, while their children were locked in another room. He allowed these victims to live. The next woman he strangled, cutting off a body part as a souvenir but then flushed it down the toilet. Another victim had pushed a chair against her door to keep the local killer out. But he'd come in through a window, killed her, and moved the chair aside to leave.

Krajcir indicates that he will spend the remainder of his days in prison counseling young incarcerated sex offenders. He's been through therapy sessions, which he claims have helped him (despite still having no idea why he did what he did). Unfortunately, an offender with no personal insight and plenty of self-pity is hardly a good role model for those who might get out of prison, as he did, to offend in the future. According to a psychologist's report, he basically blames his mother. She married a construction worker when he was four, which made the family more mobile. He also said (and the self-report of a serial killer is always suspect and self-serving) that she dressed inappropriately around the home, which sexually stimulated him, so his assaults on other women were fueled by a mix of love and anger. "I've been twisted my whole life," he said.

Although Krajcir insists he killed only Rupp in Pennsylvania, several other unsolved cases fit his MO, so he remains a suspect in them. Investigators are currently examining the possibility that Krajcir is guilty of more killings than he's admitting.

The next most heinous category of killer is the cold-blooded mass murderer and the Valley has witnessed the acts of one such person. In addition, there have been other types of multiple murders of people unrelated to the offender, so we turn now to these cases.

PART IV: MULTIPLE HITS

Dance With The Devil

It was a summer day at Lookout Point, a popular meeting place on the Lehigh University campus on the north slope of South Mountain. Late in the evening of June 30, 1995, around 9:30 P.M., two teenage girls, known to be best friends since childhood, were found shot multiple times. One was inside a red Camero, behind the wheel, and the other sprawled on a grassy area. While there were early notions that this incident might have been a murder-suicide, the conclusion was that both had been murdered. Whether it was a random hit on girls in the wrong place at the wrong time, or something more sinister was not yet determined. The victims were fifteen-year-old Mary Orlando and seventeen-year-old Jennifer Grider. They had borrowed a family car to go out for the evening and were last seen when they purchased fast food at a hamburger stand in Allentown around 9:00 P.M.. Autopsies indicated they'd been killed at Lookout Point, shot with a 9-mm handgun.

Lookout Point

The reason why the girls had been targeted remained unclear. Articles ran in the *Morning Call* about a lack of motive or suspect, and no weapon had turned up, either. The girls apparently had taken their hamburger purchase to the area, a known hangout, because the food was found with the bodies. People who lived in the area had heard screams and the sound of gunshots just before 9:30 P.M. Friends and family assured investigators that the girls had no enemies and did not hang out with bad people. Jennifer had hoped for a career in law enforcement, while Mary enjoyed dance. There seemed to be no reason why they would have been targets. Neither had been robbed or sexually assaulted. Both were from a

Bethlehem neighborhood south of the river. Mary's father and brother had already passed away. She was buried near them.

A local boxing champion from Easton offered a $5000 reward to help shake loose some tips that would lead to an arrest. Yet it was six months before an arrest was finally made, based on an anonymous tip that led to people who knew more than they'd said thus far. A young man who knew both girls well (thought to be Mary's boyfriend), who was later committed for psychiatric treatment, told police that an adolescent dealer named Christopher Bissey had gone in search of Jennifer that night because she owed him $400 for cocaine (something her family vehemently denied). With him were James Lewis and Nicolas Stroble. All three had been smoking marijuana that evening, so when they caught up to the girls the young men were high. When no money was forthcoming, Bissey apparently grew angry and started shooting, killing both girls. Several witnesses, who testified at trial, said they later heard Bissey bragging at an LSD party about the shooting. (His attorney said these people had all been hallucinating at the time.) Lewis and Stroble testified that they had seen Bissey shoot the girls, despite another young man claiming that Lewis had said Bissey was innocent. There was no murder weapon and no physical evidence to present to the jury.

Nevertheless, after only two hours of deliberation, the jury convicted Bissey of two counts of first-degree murder. He started to cry and begged that his life be spared. Although Northampton County DA John Morganelli sought the death penalty, Bissey received two life sentences. Apparently one juror had dissented, while the others had agreed he should be executed.

Despite legal concerns noted by his attorney, Bissey remains in prison. Yet there, he's been creative. To the horror of the victims' friends and family, he became lead singer of a prison rock group, "Dark Mischief," and VH-1 filmed them for "Music Behind Bars." Despite murdering two girls, he gets to revel in fame as a criminal that he probably would never have otherwise achieved.

For many who knew the victims, this murder seems entirely senseless. The same can be said for the next incident, which had an even more offensive perpetrator. He'd plague the Valley for years.

D-Day

The village of Bath, just north of Bethlehem on Route 512, is so small a driver who blinked might miss it. The area was considered quiet and safe in 1986, which might explain why few were prepared for what happened near Bath that summer. On the morning of Friday, June 6—payday for many residents—two young men with evil intent drove up to the First National Bank in a brown Monte Carlo. Martin Daniel Appel, 27, was the mastermind who had promised his dim-witted partner, Stanley Hertzog, plenty of money.

Marty Appel

The narcissistic Appel reportedly viewed himself as a genius. A World War II buff, he had hefty aspirations to *be* somebody, but not much ability to follow through. Deep in debt, he lived in a trailer five miles from the bank.

Branch manager Marcia Hauser, 31, had recently opened for business, and two bank tellers and a customer service representative were set up and ready for customers. For three of them, this was to be their last day alive.

Appel and Hertzog drove around the bank to examine it from all sides. They wanted to be certain the conditions were right. At first, there were too many customers, but eventually only a few cars remained, and Appel knew which belonged to the bank's employees. He'd already checked the layout to ensure he'd know who stood where and how to take command of the place. He knew the tellers had no means of protection. To create a diversion for the state troopers and local police, Appel first went to a local restaurant to report that a bomb would soon go off in the local airport some distance away. Then he carefully parked his car in the bank's lot to facilitate their getaway.

Armed with a concealed 9-mm automatic and a Colt .38 revolver, the two men entered the bank. Each approached a teller to pretend to make a transaction. Suddenly, Appel made his move. He pulled out his gun and wounded one teller and killed the other. He turned and shot across the room at the customer service rep, Jane Hartman, along with her customer, Thomas Marchetto, a former marine, wounding both. Ms. Hartman took cover under the desk. Then he shot at the bank manager, but she, too, escaped. Fearing he'd left witnesses, Appel crossed to the customer service area and shot Ms. Hartman under the desk, this time killing her. He shot Marchetto again, but still only wounded him. Hertzog, who apparently wasn't that clear about the plan, went after the manager, shooting her a number of times, while Appel returned to the first wounded teller and "put her out of her misery." Both tellers and the customer service rep now lay dead.

The men hastily grabbed some money and fled, getting only about $2,280. They were unaware that they'd left two witnesses wounded but alive, as well as two employees who'd been in a back room. These two saw Appel drive away on Route 329, and they urged the bank custodian, who had just arrived, to follow the car. He did so, catching up when Appel and Hertzog were delayed by a slow tractor trailer, which allowed him to record most of the license plate number.

A call went out immediately to all area police departments, who set up roadblocks around the county, while emergency personnel responded to the scene inside the bank. Marchetto and Hauser were transported to hospitals, the other three to the morgue. Family members were notified.

Within hours of the robbery, the outlaws were captured. They had hidden their guns and changed their clothes, but the car was easy to identify. Despite their short-lived celebration of their own brand of a "D-Day Invasion," they hadn't managed to achieve much to brag about. When they heard reports about how much information the police had, they went out to dump some incriminating items and came square against a roadblock. Knowing they had nowhere to go, they surrendered, but were prepared with a fabricated story.

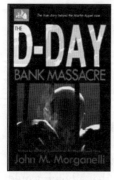

The DA who inherited the case, John Morganelli, also wrote *The D-Day Bank Massacre*. He relied on statements given by Appel, as well as court records. Under questioning, both men said they had been in the car in the vicinity of the bank that morning, which explained why witnesses saw them, but they claimed to have no knowledge of a robbery.

Police accompanied them to Appel's trailer for a search, and several guns found in odd hiding places were confiscated for ballistics testing. The suspects continued to assert their innocence, but by early evening the tests confirmed that the weapons had been used at the bank to shoot and kill people. Even then, Appel denied he was involved. However, the stolen money turned up in his refrigerator, wrapped in foil. Inside the car were coin drawers missing from the bank.

Appel and Hertzog were then transported to the state trooper barracks and charged with three counts of homicide, two counts of aggravated assault and attempted murder, one count of robbery, and six counts of criminal conspiracy. They were held without bail at the Northampton County Prison. Appel asked for a lawyer, but shortly after he was arraigned, on June 9, he said he wanted to make a full confession. This sounded too good to be true, and it was, but no one would realize this for years.

On videotape, Appel told how he had carefully prepared for the bank robbery and had intended to kill all witnesses; there should have been five people dead, not three. He and Hertzog had actually broken into the bank early one morning the week before to study its layout, taking nothing at the time but destroying equipment. Appel had also estimated how long it would take the nearest police to arrive on the scene.

His account took about an hour and Appel assured the police that the plan had been his alone, including the elimination of witnesses. He mentioned the significance of the D-Day anniversary. He'd done most of the shooting, he said, and when asked if he was aware that what he had done was wrong, he admitted he was, adding that the massacre had simply been necessary to remove obstacles to his personal enrichment. To everyone who watched his cold narrative, he seemed clear-headed, articulate, and willing to cooperate. While this was the worst massacre in the county's history, the DA thought it would be a relatively straightforward process to resolve it and punish the offenders. But the authorities had not counted on state politics or on just how clever Martin Appel was. He might not have been a genius in his overall plan, but once caught, he watched for a way to work the system to his own advantage.

Hertzog consulted with an attorney and insisted he was not guilty and wanted a trial. Appel, on the other hand, stated that he expected to be executed and even wanted to die in the electric chair. He rejected the assistance of an attorney and told Judge Robert A. Freedberg that he wanted to represent himself, in part because he believed only he could fully express his ideas and in part because an attorney would slow the process. The judge described the charges and penalties. Appel insisted he fully understood.

To cover all bases, Judge Freedberg ordered a psychiatric examination to ensure that Appel was competent to waive counsel and defend himself. Appel was examined by a board-certified psychiatrist, Dr. Janet Schwartz, who concluded he was competent: He demonstrated no thought disorders that she could see and his intelligence level was above average. She said he had made a rational decision to accept the death penalty: He wanted to die because he did not wish to spend the rest of his life in prison. He had a B.A. in psychology and had served in the army, receiving a dishonorable discharge for going AWOL. At the time of the robbery, he'd been working as a cab driver, although he was a former prison guard (fired after impersonating a police officer). All of this indicated that even if he had a personality disorder, he could tell right from wrong.

Since Appel was found competent, he had the right to go *pro se*, according to the Sixth Amendment of the Constitution, i.e., to represent himself. While he was allowed to be his own attorney, two public defenders were appointed as standby counsel. That way, he could use their services if he elected to. However, until he was formally granted this status, they were responsible for seeing that he was appropriately evaluated for competence. It was this brief "limbo" period that later became an issue.

Back in prison, Appel began a campaign of letter writing, wherein he told law enforcement he could get his cohort, Hertzog, to confess. He asked for some time alone with Hertzog, after which he'd be ready to testify against him. Ostensibly, Appel wanted the entire thing over with as soon as possible. He waived several hearings in order to accelerate the process. He also gave another confession, reiterating the details on tape in a consistent manner and stated he'd have shot anyone else he saw. The other two employees had just been lucky.

At one point, Appel insisted he wanted to waive a trial and plead guilty. He definitely wanted the death penalty, saying his death might atone for the lives he had taken, and adding that if he were to receive a life sentence, guards would die in his attempts to escape. In fact, not only did he want to die, but he asked to be executed within the next six months. This way, he could gain a little slice of fame as the first person to be executed in Pennsylvania since 1962.

For a third time, Appel said he wished to plead guilty and waive counsel, and he asked that the judge decide the case and impose the sentence. He even thanked everyone involved.

On August 7, and for two more days, Judge Freedberg commenced a hearing on Appel's degree of guilt. The DA's office presented witnesses and exhibits to affirm a first-degree, pre-meditated triple homicide, while Appel offered no one to speak on his behalf. Judge Freedberg found Appel guilty and asked again if he wished to have a jury decide the sentence. He declined, stating he would make no appeal. He also asked that no right-to-life groups file appeals on his behalf.

While his determination to die was unusual, it was not unprecedented. In 1930 Carl Panzram, who claimed to have killed 21 people, acted as his own attorney to ensure that he would be convicted of another murder and be given the death penalty. He was hanged. In the 1970s in Utah, Gary Gilmore, who had killed two men in cold blood, accepted the court's decision to impose the death penalty. He wanted no appeals and fought off groups and individuals that tried to stay his execution. He was executed by firing squad in 1977. In both cases, the offenders had decided they did not wish to spend years incarcerated, as they had already spent most of their lives in some form of detention.

Appel made no final arguments and affirmed again that he wanted the death penalty, so his wish was granted. To ensure that he was of sound mind, Appel's standby counsel had both a psychiatrist and a psychologist examine him again. Neither found any psychological disorders, although he was viewed as grandiose, compartmentalized and cold-blooded.

"It would appear that the Appel case should have been an easy one for the prosecution," writes DA John Morganelli. "After all, Appel robbed a bank, murdered three people in cold blood, seriously wounded two others, and did so in full view of a number of witnesses who survived to tell about it. Moreover, Appel had confessed on videotape and explained in detail how he planned the crime and executed it." Appel had even agreed that he deserved death. He'd been examined by three mental health professionals and the judge had given him every chance to change his mind.

However, at this point politics changed the game. Pennsylvania law required a review of all death penalty cases, so its Supreme Court examined the evidence, the way the sentence had been imposed, the aggravating circumstances that justified death, and whether the sentence fit the crime. No one had been executed in Pennsylvania for over two decades, so they wanted to be very careful.

During this time, a television network offered Appel $50,000 for his story and he prepared to marry his girlfriend, so she would inherit it. It was at this point that his first calculated maneuver took place. He offered his testimony against Hertzog in exchange for an "intimate" period with his fiancée. Although no one approved the request, he gave testimony anyway, assuming the deal was done. During Hertzog's trial, Appel offered several important facts: Hertzog had lent him the money for his gun, had stated he could kill people, and had suggested a diversionary plan for the date of the robbery. The jury convicted Hertzog of first-degree murder, and he received a life sentence.

Appel gave his TV interview and offered more to local reporters... for a price. He hinted he was frustrated that he'd not yet received the intimate visit he wanted with his fiancée and that he might stop cooperating. He even told Hertzog's counsel that the DA had coached him on what to say in Hertzog's trial. Trouble was clearly brewing. Appel offered to assist in obtaining a new trial for his partner, stating that Hertzog had killed no one and should not be punished as if he had.

Admitting perjury (which cost him nothing), Appel now provided reasons at a hearing why Hertzog should receive a new trial. Apparently, this was his return volley for what he perceived as the DA's betrayal. But a new trial for Hertzog was denied, while Appel's death sentence was upheld. His file went to then-Governor Robert Casey, who delayed signing the death warrant. No one from Northampton County could get him to budge, so Appel began writing letters threatening to expose the governor's reticence. Three years had passed since the Bath massacre without any significant movement. Appel gave more interviews in which he affirmed that he had known what he was doing and had viewed his victims as expendable. He had no remorse.

Governor Casey's first term ended and Appel's death warrant remained unsigned. Casey's reelection meant even more delays. Yet Appel insisted he still wanted to follow through. However, it's likely that at this point, if not before, he was just lying. He'd recently had surgery for an overactive thyroid, and that event would soon figure into how the tables were about to turn.

Morganelli made an unprecedented move, as he recounts it, and filed a lawsuit to compel the governor to act. Close to eight years after the crime, the Commonwealth Court voted in favor of commanding Casey to sign the warrant. But Casey appealed, gaining more time. The appeal was denied and he was given sixty days to comply. He appealed to a higher court, but by now his term was over. Tom Ridge defeated Casey's chosen successor, and on February 28, 1995, he signed the warrant and assigned a date for execution. Martin Appel was scheduled to die on April 4.

That's when the fireworks began. Appel now requested legal assistance to stop the execution. He had played the system, getting plenty of attention, and now he was going to turn it all around. He received a stay of execution, so his attorneys could prepare. Judge Freedberg ordered all records to be given to them, and soon the basis for the appeal emerged: Appel had suffered most of his life from an overactive thyroid, which he claimed had made him delusional, so all of the decisions he'd made, including the one to confess, were subject to evaluation for incompetence. In short, he was now angling for an insanity defense.

In addition, Appel's attorneys claimed that the state had failed to produce evidence that potentially exonerated him—his psychiatric records—and had denied him appropriate access to legal counsel. Given how much everyone had extended themselves in 1986 and thereafter to cover all these bases, the claims seemed ludicrous. Yet, Appel's new attorneys were quite serious.

"Appel was psychotic and delusional," said Rob Dunham. According to the *New York Times*, Dunham worked for the Pennsylvania Capital Case Resource Center, an anti-death penalty organization that assisted convicted felons with the process of getting a stay of execution. On Appel's behalf, they said they wanted to vacate all legal decisions and start over.

Thanks to legal precedent, Judge Freedberg had little choice but to do it. Under the assumption that while Appel had been delusional during earlier proceedings, he was not delusional with this post-surgical filing for post-conviction relief, so he had to be given the benefit of the doubt—even a small percentage of doubt. Paradoxical as it all seemed, Appel's ploy was exceedingly clever, and demonstrated both the egocentric and remorseless nature of a psychopathic personality. He had no regard for what he was putting his surviving victims and the victims' families through, just as he'd earlier had no regard for the victims. There was no reason to believe, despite all his talk of atonement, that he cared about anyone but himself.

An expert testified that Appel had had Grave's Disease, which can sometimes produce psychotic states, and Appel's girlfriend affirmed his obsession with World War II (although she admitted that his "delusional" statements had started only after he was arrested). When Appel had "trained" Hertzog to go into the "mission" with him, he supposedly saw himself as a general commanding a soldier. (One source states that after Appel was caught, he'd offered himself to the CIA for a suicide mission, to make his death worth something.)

However, there was no evidence that Appel had suffered any psychotic manifestations of Grave's Disease; he'd only complained of heart palpitations. In addition, Hertzog testified that while Appel had been "weird," it was clear to him that the robbery had not been about a CIA operation, but rather about getting money to pay off debts and purchase things for his girlfriend. If he couldn't buy her stuff, he was afraid he'd lose her.

Experts for the prosecution reviewed all the psychiatric evaluations, convinced that everything had been done properly and thoroughly. There was no indication from any prison records that Appel had exhibited psychotic symptoms. One psychologist noted sociopathic features and criminal goals, and another stated that while no tests had revealed mental illness, one showed a high score for psychopathic behavior. Appel's selective manner of revealing his supposed CIA link indicated controlled calculation, not delusion. Another professional explained that, in any event, delusional behavior did not necessarily imply incompetence to participate in legal proceedings. In addition, there had been no symptoms from Grave's Disease in 1986.

The court dismissed Appel's contention that he was incompetent in 1986 and vacated the stay of execution. He was eligible to appeal this decision, and he did. Appel first took his case to the Pennsylvania Supreme Court, but in 1997, these justices unanimously upheld Judge Freedberg's decision. This didn't stop him; Appel went higher yet. Morganelli points out that recent changes in the law had made it more difficult for federal courts to second-guess state courts and "substitute their judgments," but this depended on how determined any given judge might be. The death penalty was always a hot potato, no matter how certain the guilt.

Billy Nolas and Robert Dunham from the Pennsylvania Capital Case Resource Center filed a petition to the federal court for the Eastern District of Pennsylvania. It went through several stages, focusing on the issue that Appel's 1986 attorneys

—the standby counsel—had not fully investigated the possibility of incompetence before he'd been allowed to represent himself. They had not asked enough questions of his parents and girlfriend, who apparently knew more than they had said. As such, U.S. District Judge William Yohn, Jr. decided Appel had been deprived of legal counsel.

In the spring of 1999, nearly thirteen years after the massacre that had shocked the Valley, the court ruled that Appel had not been competent in 1986 to act as his own attorney. Thus, his conviction and death sentence were vacated, and Appel was now eligible for a new trial, which had to commence within six months. Since a number of key witnesses were now dead and an insanity defense loomed, DA Morganelli met with the families most centrally involved and learned from them that they just wanted closure, whatever it took. A plea deal appeared to be the best way.

In 2001 Appel, now 42, pled guilty and received three life sentences, plus 42 to 84 years on other charges. Morganelli, disheartened by the process, wrote, "His case is illustrative of the obstacles the system has in place for prosecutors in our attempt to convict and punish society's worst offenders." Judge Freedberg stated that Appel was "perhaps the worst offender this court has ever had before it." Relatives of the victims, too, believed that the system had worked for the offender and against the interests of the community. But at least the literary community had not been snowed. Apparently Appel tried getting some literary agents interested in his own book on the incident (and himself as the star), but none bit. Yet.

While this triple homicide, with two additional victims, was a shock to the Valley, most residents know that the drug trade has infiltrated the area. With it have come drug-related executions, including a recent incident that appears to have ties to local drug runners.

West Ward Triple

A triple homicide occurred in a building in Easton on November 29, 2007, on the 100 block of North 13th Street. Police received a report about a post-midnight disturbance and in a second-floor bedroom responding officers found the bodies of two women and a man. All three had been shot. A man who lived in the home and who had called it in, gave police a false name, but he was soon correctly identified. Since this was a potential obstruction of justice, he was charged. Officers noted that the building was in an area where drugs were sold. The victims were soon identified as Chanel Armour, 23, Aleah Hamlin, 19, and Alphe Rene, 21. They were visiting a woman who had retired to the third floor that night with her children. Apparently all had been asleep when someone entered the home and shot the three on the second floor. The incident appeared to be target-specific and planned. Information turned up that one of the female victims had confided to relatives that a man had threatened to kill her.

71

The police quickly developed three suspects, all of them black males involved in running drugs between Easton, New Jersey, and New York. Investigators spotted a connection with a collection of people they'd already been watching who'd been selling cocaine to street dealers in Easton. Federal agents had joined state and local police as part of the Route 222 Corridor Anti-Gang Initiative, and some members of this million-dollar-a-year ring were suspects in other murders. In mid-March 2008, the task force made its move, raiding drug dens across Easton to terminate the operation. Twenty-six people were indicted and ten more charged with possession. Among them were people whom the authorities believed had information about several murders, including the triple homicide.

Erick Casimir had been slain in February 2006, also in the West Ward, and he'd been dating one of the dealers arrested. Another dealer pled guilty to that murder. A small-time dealer named Marcellus McDuffie had been gunned down in May 2006, outside an Easton restaurant, for which gang member Andrew Paschal was convicted. He was related to one of the suspects recently indicted.

Then, at the end of March 2008, DA Morganelli announced the arrest of two men, one from New Jersey, who were firm suspects in the triple homicide. He added that two more were being sought. Since the case is pending, we'll give no names, but it's become paramount for local authorities to show gangs and drug runners they cannot just invade communities and kill people at whim—not even other dealers.

For our final part, we turn to homicidal hits, random or otherwise, and murders long unsolved.

PART V: RANDOM HITS AND COLD CASES

Bizarre Circumstances

On Saturday afternoon, March 7, 1953, the bodies of Gail and Paul Schultz were found face down in Black Rock Creek, behind the East Lawn Gardens subdivision of Nazareth. Gail, 18, had been taking her twelve-year-old half-brother who was mentally-handicapped for a walk. They stopped by a friend's house, but the friend could not join them, so they went to the creek alone. A high school graduate, Gail devoted herself to caring for Paul Jr. Her mother had died when Gail was a child. Her father had gotten remarried to a woman named Claire. Gail liked to teach Paul things and had dressed him in rubber boots that day for their nature lesson.

Claire grew worried when they had not returned by 4:30 P.M. She sent Paul Sr. out to call for them and when they failed to respond he walked about five hundred feet to the creek. From the window Claire could see him bend over and pick up one of the children, so she rushed out to see. To their horror, Gail and Paul had been lying not far from the house all this time, in ten inches of water. The gash on Gail's forehead indicated she'd hit her head on a rock. They surmised that young Paul had fallen first and Gail had slipped in her effort to rescue him. Paul tried administering mouth-to-mouth resuscitation as a friend called an ambulance. The ambulance crew attempted to revive the children, as did volunteers at a local fire company. But it was too late.

The bodies were taken to a hospital, where a quick autopsy indicated they'd died around the time they'd left their friend's house—about 2:30 P.M. They were transported to a funeral home to be prepared for a viewing. It was there that funeral director John C. Kalina noticed that their head wounds were too severe and too oddly shaped to have been caused by a fall. One puncture had penetrated Paul Jr.'s skull. Kalina was the first person to notify the police. A more thorough examination indicated that both children had been struck on the head with a blunt instrument, like a hammer. This was not a freak accident, but a double homicide. Gail had been hit seven times, Paul three, and Gail's thumb was fractured, as if she were trying to protect herself. It seemed impossible, but this shocking attack had occurred in the middle of a sunny afternoon, right under their parents' noses and within eyesight of a dozen homes. Yet no one had seen a thing.

The perpetrator, whoever he was, had a good head start. In fact, the state police had no inkling about the incident until a reporter called them. By then, the murder site had been unsecured for hours and trampled by many different people. It was virtually useless for an investigation, and darkness now hindered arriving police. When they returned in the morning, two inches of snow obliterated the landscape.

Gail's glasses were only forty feet away from where she'd been found, but it would be nine days before anyone saw them. No murder weapon was located at the scene.

The police file on the unsolved case is over four hundred pages long, consisting largely of interview transcripts (including with all known sexual deviants as far away as Philadelphia), the coroner's inquest, a succession of tips from over the years, and old photos. One witness report came from a railroad man on a train passing through who recalled a man in a tan raincoat in the area. Others had seen a teenage boy wandering around. However, no leads panned out, despite a reward and the work of a private investigator and a prominent criminologist from Chicago. One neighbor had remained inside his home during all the excitement and had no clear alibi for himself during the time of the murder, so he became the first viable suspect. After he passed a lie detector test and successfully endured two days of interrogation, he was released.

The following year, Paul Sr., only 48, suffered a heart attack and died. Claire Schultz sold the home and moved away.

In 1988, 35 years later, relatives posted a reward for information when they realized there was still interest in the case, but as yet it remains unsolved.

Treasure Hunt

The *New York Times* laid out the facts in 1991, when the Boston Museum of Fine Arts was haggling with Lafayette College over who owned a rare piece of Egyptian art. This piece also figured into a murder mystery in the Valley, thanks to a thousand-page diary about a romantic affair.

Lafayette Library

Alice Hall was a librarian at Lafayette College for many years. In 1984, she was found stabbed to death in her home in Palmer Township. In her diary, which ran from 1960 into the 1970s, she described an affair she was having with the head librarian, Clyde Haselden, who had hired her. They often when on discreet "business" trips together, and while she wasn't particularly happy with the way he'd

74

treat her at times, she nevertheless wanted to marry him. After his wife died in 1982, she pressured him, but he later claimed he'd told her it was too soon to consider marriage again. Not long afterward, she was dead and he became a suspect.

Hairs found in the home were consistent with his, but he'd been a frequent visitor, so that meant little. Since the police had no other evidence against Haselden, a month later, the seventy-year-old man moved south. Special Agent Ronald P. Walker from the FBI's Behavioral Sciences Unit prepared a profile of the type of person who had killed Alice. While this person may seem outwardly calm, the agent wrote, he would have inner turmoil. Acquaintances would notice his sudden insomnia, agitation, change in eating habits, and erratic temper. Walker believed Alice had died during an emotional confrontation when "something went wrong in an existing relationship." This profile, however, got investigators no closer to solving the crime. The case went cold, but interest was revived again in the wake of the museum scandal.

Seven years before the murder, in 1977, a 3,600 year-old glass-studded, silver and gold pectoral breastplate from a royal sarcophagus had been stolen from the library. However, no one noticed until it resurfaced in 1987, mentioned in a letter by another researcher. The librarians learned that the missing piece had been purchased in 1980 by the Boston Museum of Fine Art at a Sotheby's auction, offered by a Tinicum Township antiques dealer on behalf of a private client. It sold for $165,000.

Some surmised that Alice was killed because she knew about the theft and had threatened to expose it.

Lafayette College demanded to have it back, but the Boston Museum, which had restored it, was unwilling to turn it over, especially since Lafayette had done nothing over the past decade to report it or look for it. Lafayette responded that the thief had taken it from a vault where it was stored and had destroyed the records. (The college had purchased it in 1873 for $425 from the widow of a man who'd bought it in Egypt.)

It turned out that the antiques dealer's client was former assistant Lafayette librarian Robert G. Gennett. He admitted he'd stolen the breastplate, but he named no accomplices—neither Haselden nor Hall. He was ordered to pay more than $100,000 to cover the college's legal costs. It was decided in court that the museum would keep the royal breastplate, but pay the college an undisclosed sum. There was never any proven connection to the murder of Alice Hall, and that case remains unsolved.

Family Tragedies

The doorbell rang at Moira "Holly" Branagan's upscale home in Bethlehem on March 28, 1979. The seventeen-year-old was talking to a friend on the phone and excused herself to go answer the door. She returned and told her friend that she would call back to talk about their dinner plans, but that call never came. Holly's brother Sean, a freshman at Lehigh University, tried calling all day and got only a busy signal. Concerned, he came home the next day. Sean found Holly face down on the kitchen floor with a ten-inch knife in her back. W. Richard Branagan, their father, was away on a business trip. He'd lost his wife to cancer only two years earlier, so this new blow was doubly difficult.

The police arrived and processed the scene, but the offender had either wiped the knife clean of fingerprints or worn gloves. Since it was from the home and there was no evidence of forced entry, the incident seemed more a crime of passion than a planned attack. Yet Holly had not been sexually assaulted and nothing appeared to have been taken from the home, so the motive remained a mystery. Holly, a soccer player and choir member, had no known enemies and was not hanging out with a bad crowd. Even so, some investigators believed she knew her attacker.

Sean had been with a friend that afternoon, so he was cleared, and the person with whom Holly had been speaking on the phone was aware she was home alone. The doorbell had rung about 4:30 P.M. and Holly had called her father's office from her bedroom about fifteen minutes later, leaving the phone off the hook. Those who knew her believed she would not have allowed a stranger inside while there alone, and she would have seen who was at the door through the front windows.

According to Coroner Joe Reichel, the autopsy indicated she'd been stabbed at least fifteen times. There were also defensive wounds on her hands, and three minor cuts in other areas.

Investigators developed leads and even traveled out of state, but each lead ended without a resolution. Even psychics offered help, including the "Amazing Kreskin," but none managed to provide the right information. Kreskin used a technique he called "stimulation of the imagination" to interview people, including the girl who'd been talking with Holly on the phone that day. She was able to recall the songs playing on the radio in the background, and with assistance from the station, they pinned down a time-of-death determination.

Then Mr. Branagan sustained yet another terrible blow. Only a few months after Holly's murder, on the morning of September 9, 1979, Sean was working at a gas station in Hanover Township. A spark from a cleaning machine ignited gasoline fumes and in the resulting explosion, Sean and another young man were critically burned. Sean died in the hospital. In short order, Mr. Branagan had lost his entire family.

In 1981, Bethlehem police received a tip from a private investigator that a prison inmate, Michael Jezick, knew who had killed Holly. He claimed he'd been present when it happened, describing an older man who was a petty thief and drug dealer. However, investigators turned up no physical evidence to corroborate his statement. In 1986, the FBI's Behavioral Science Unit offered a profile based on evidence from the crime scene, but this, too, failed to move the case along. Mr. Branagan eventually left the area and Holly's murder went unsolved.

Full Disclosure

Not far away, on the campus of Lehigh University, a young woman was murdered in her dorm room in April 1986. Jeanne Ann Clery, 19, was asleep in her room when another student, Joseph Henry, broke in around 6:00 A.M., burglarized her room, then raped her, strangled her, and cut her throat. Apparently, some residents had propped open the dorm's entrance doors to sneak in their boyfriends, but others, like Henry, could also gain access. The school's patrol apparently failed to secure the doors that night, although they were aware of the practice of "propping." According to the *New York Times*, school officials had known that Henry, there on a full scholarship, had disciplinary problems. A drug abuser, he bragged to four others the next day about what he'd done and one of them told the police. Henry was arrested, tried, convicted, and sentenced to die in the electric chair.

Jeanne Clery

Jeanne's parents, Connie and Howard Clery, were stunned, but rather than remain immobilized with grief, they did some research and learned about three dozen incidents of violent crime on the Lehigh campus over the prior two years, half of which had been committed by Lehigh students. No one had ever informed them of this, instead presenting the campus as a safe haven. There wasn't even a policy for punishing students caught propping doors. The Clerys sued the school for $25 million, arguing that security measures at their daughter's dorm and around campus had been inadequate. For the safety of future students, they wanted Lehigh to put electronically monitored locks on dormitory entrances, increase security guards, and limit access to the dorms at night to a single main entrance that could be properly monitored.

After settling their suit, Jeanne's parents developed a national campaign to increase awareness about crime on college campuses. They provided statistics to prove that campuses around the country were not safe havens—some crimes actually occurred at higher rates on campuses—and demanded that administrative attitudes that protected school reputations change. Only then would security tighten around the country. The Clerys' campaign inspired the Pennsylvania Legislature to require that all campuses, public or private, publish crime statistics in their admissions literature, as well as policies for dealing with students who had a criminal record or were caught committing a crime. Eventually, the Clery Act became a landmark federal law, tying participation to federal financial aid. Any school that failed to comply could be fined by the U. S. Department of Education. In 1992, victims rights measures were added, and in 1998, reporting requirements were expanded. For more information, the Clerys offer a Web site, "What Jeanne Didn't Know," at: http://www.securityoncampus.org/aboutsoc/didntknow.html.

The Missingest Man

One of the enduring mysteries from out of the Lehigh Valley is that of Judge Joseph Force Crater. Born in 1889 in Easton, he grew up there and attended Lafayette College before going off to earn a degree from Columbia University Law School.

Judge Crater

He took up the practice of law in New York and became president of the Democratic Party Club. However, there was plenty of political corruption in those days and the Judge's success could well have been entangled in it. Spring of 1930, then-Governor Franklin D. Roosevelt appointed him as Associate Judge of the New York Supreme Court. Just days before the appointment was announced, he withdrew a considerable amount of money from his bank account—$20,000—just right for the standard bribe for corrupt local officials in Tammany Hall who had sponsored him.

During July of 1930, Judge Crater was with his wife at their vacation home at Belgrade Lakes, Maine, when he received a phone call. The Judge informed his wife he had business in the city, but did not identify the caller or reveal what he was about to go do. He merely said something about having to "straighten those fellows out." Circumstances suggest the caller was a show girl with whom he was having an affair, as he subsequently accompanied her on an overnight excursion to Atlantic City. He then returned to Maine before taking the last trip of his life back to Manhattan.

There followed a series of unexplained transactions that support the idea that Judge Crater was being extorted or that he planned to walk away from his life into a new one, possibly with a new woman. The last known sighting, at least for many decades, was of Judge Crater leaving a restaurant on August 6, 1930. He seemed to be in good spirits and he waved to friends with whom he'd dined before hailing a cab. He was wearing a double-breasted brown suit, a straw Panama hat, and a high-collared shirt.

At first, no one missed him. It was over a week before his wife began calling friends and acquaintances, and only when Crater failed to show up for the opening of the courts did people realize he was truly missing. It was then learned that on the day he disappeared, he had gone through his files and asked his assistant, Joseph Mara, to cash two large checks for him, to the tune of over $5000. He also took $20,000 from campaign funds. Around noon, he and Mara carried two briefcases to his Manhattan apartment.

Crater purchased a ticket to a Broadway play that evening, called "Dancing Partners," and went out to dinner. Running into friends, he missed the show's opening, so he took his leave and stepped into a cab.

The police investigation that September turned up no leads, and the story became a media sensation: Prominent judge virtually disappears. His safe deposit box was empty and the two briefcases that Mara described were gone. As with many high profile cases, leads poured in from all over the world, most of them false, but the city's resources were taxed to the max. A grand jury called 95 witnesses, but there was too little evidence to form an opinion about what had happened to the man. He could be dead, he could be alive. He could be wandering around with amnesia. No one knew. But one thing was certain: if he was alive, he knew that a lot of people were looking for him.

In the New York apartment, Sally Crater found uncashed checks, stocks, bonds, and a note to the effect that Crater had been wary of someone, but he named no one. She believed he'd been the victim of foul play. It took a decade, but in 1939, Judge Crater was officially declared deceased. His case was closed 40 years later. Theories were spun for years afterward about what became New York's longest-running missing persons case, but in 2005, an announcement was made that the case might finally have been cracked.

The NYPD Cold Case Squad investigated a letter left behind by Stella Ferrucci-Good, who died April 2, 2005, that claimed she knew what had happened to the good judge. Her granddaughter found the letter, along with a metal box full of clippings about Crater's disappearance, but the envelope warned not to open it until her death. Stella's own husband, Parks Department Supervisor Robert Good (now deceased), was in on it, she said. With an NYPD cop named Charles Burns and the cop's brother, cabby Frank Burns, he'd allegedly killed the judge and buried his body beneath the boardwalk at West Eighth Street in Coney Island. It was now the site of an aquarium, and in fact, the skeletal remains of five bodies had been unearthed during the 1950s when the ground was excavated to start work on the aquarium. Sources also confirmed that a police officer named Robert Burns had served during the right period of time at the precinct at Coney Island. However, the exhumed bones had all been moved to a potter's field on Hart Island, and over the decades had mingled with other unclaimed remains, so it's unlikely there will ever be a definitive answer as to whether the "missingest man in New York" was killed, and if so, why.

Another unsolved historic case involved a local businessman.

The Strange Case of Monroe Snyder

Before the Hill-to-Hill bridge was built, a covered bridge connected south and north Bethlehem. On this bridge, one night in February 1873, the night watchman came across Monroe Snyder, who claimed to be wounded. Yet there was no blood and the fifty-five-year-old man seemed able to walk away on his own. However, the following day, Snyder's body was discovered in the Monacacy Creek, his head crushed and his body pierced with multiple stab wounds. The coroners from Northampton and Lehigh Counties argued over jurisdiction, since he apparently lay directly on the county line, but since his head was in Lehigh, that coroner got the case.

And a difficult case it was, with multiple suspects who apparently overheard the businessman speaking quite loudly about his financial affairs while on a train to New York. In addition, he was well insured, with his son the beneficiary. There was evidence that he was despondent over his debts and that he had insured himself so that, should something happen to him, all could be paid off. In other words, there were a lot of possibilities, including suicide: He might have stabbed himself and jumped from the bridge, hitting his head. However, the final decision, thanks to evidence that he had been dragged to the creek, was that his death was a homicide. A knife was found in the creek, although it was the head wound that had been fatal.

Despite all the early leads, no evidence ever tied anyone to this murder, and the detective involved remained convinced it had been a suicide. However, the life insurance company, which would not pay the benefit in the event Snyder had taken his own life, finally settled with the man's family.

Telling Evidence

In Easton's hundred–acre cemetery at 401 North Seventh Street, more than 29,000 people have been buried, the first one on All Saint's Day, November 1, 1849. Mostly it's a peaceful place, providing the sort of stroll one expects from 19th century garden cemeteries. Reputed to be haunted, this burial ground was also the scene of a high profile body dump.

During the spring of 1996, thirteen-year-old Richezza Williams ran away from her home on Long Island. Her family reported her missing on March 19, but she was spotted in Brooklyn on several occasions. She got involved with a gang of drug suppliers and ended up in Easton, passing herself off as "Materon Buffy Smith," telling people that she was nineteen. She lived with a man in a building that also housed a business in used furniture. In July, she disappeared.

On August 11, an eyewitness came forward to tell a terrible story: On July 28, at her house on Bushkill Street, she'd seen three men drag "Smith" into the basement. These men gathered what appeared to be instruments of torture, including hangers and a corkscrew, and then she heard the girl screaming. Eventually, the screams stopped and the men brought the girl out of the basement in a box from a kerosene heater. She was dead and they were discussing a way to get rid of the body. Nothing was said to officials until after these same three men broke into the witness's house on August 5 and tortured her and a friend with knives and heated wire hangers, apparently to intimidate them. Scared for her life, the witness finally went to the police. Her report precipitated a search for the body.

It was August 10, before the girl's decomposed remains were found in the most ignominious of places—still in the box, placed inside an old cemetery storage vault. A detective noticed a piece of chewing gum on the vault's dirty floor, so he collected it. This would prove to be a fortuitous discovery. Dr. Dennis Asen, a local forensic odontologist, made a cast of the clear teeth marks left in the gum and awaited the capture of a suspect.

Cemetery Storage Vault Where Body Was Found

Dental analysis performed on the remains indicated that this was the young runaway, Richezza Williams. She'd been burned, poked and cut with red-hot devices, after which bleach had been poured into her open wounds. However, the remains were too far gone for the pathologist to provide an accurate cause of death.

It turned out that the victim had been involved with a gang known as the Cash Money Boys, Easton's leading drug dealers, and that her crack addiction had driven her to steal $2,000 in drugs from them. They apparently tortured and murdered her as punishment and a warning to anyone else pondering such a theft.

The witness identified the men responsible and on August 12, one of them, Corey Maeweather, 19, was arrested and charged with homicide, kidnapping, aggravated assault, and conspiracy. He had recently served a sentence in Northampton County Prison for trafficking in cocaine. Dr. Asen made a cast of his mouth and found that one of his teeth fit the mold from the gum "like a lock and key." Maeweather offered a confession and pled guilty.

The police also knew the identities of his accomplices, Stanley Obas, 18, and Kwame Henry, 19. Known to be armed, they reportedly traveled often between Brooklyn and Easton. While they remained on the run for a while, issuing statements that they would not be taken without a fight, within two years Kwame Henry was caught. Tried for first-degree murder, he was convicted. He and Maeweather both received life sentences. Obas was profiled in 2001 on *America's Most Wanted,* but he remains at large.

Too Many Suspects

In October 1992, a pair of landscapers discovered the body of Jean Theresa Sufrich in a field at 9th and Linden Streets in Bethlehem Township. Someone had shot her in the head with a large-caliber gun, with an impact so great that part of her skull had flown into the overhead branches. Known to be a prostitute and substance abuser, it was difficult to learn how she met her end. But then Lori Sheirer stepped up and offered details. She had been with Sufrich on the evening she died, Sheirer admitted, and had given her money to buy heroin, but Sufrich had never come back.

The police knew Sheirer well; she liked attention and had given false leads in other cases. A victim of alleged abuse, she had attempted suicide several times and felt like a misfit. She'd also gotten into drugs.

Sheirer told police that she'd encountered two men who'd been out looking for Sufrich on the night of the murder. Then a day or so after the murder, before details were reported in the press, a man told her he knew that Sufrich had been shot in the head. However, a polygraph indicated Sheirer was making false statements. Still, she seemed to know something that no one else did, except the investigating officers.

Then they got a tip that Sheirer herself was the killer, so they interrogated her. She admitted she'd had a dream in which she and Sufrich had fought, and in the dream she had then chased Sufrich to the place where her body was found and shot her. Afterward, she cleaned herself up and went to work.

Investigators took Sheirer to the crime scene and she accurately demonstrated how the body had fallen, even when they tried tricking her with false information. She also knew the items in Sufrich's fanny pack. Later she admitted she was in fact the tipster that had sent police in her direction. She was soon under arrest, and while in prison she learned that the prosecutor was seeking the death penalty. She looked for someone to help prove she was innocent.

With Sheirer's trial in 1993, Northampton County was presented with its first defense of multiple personality disorder: Sheirer was claiming she had fabricated the story about the dream to keep the investigating state trooper interested in her.

Sheirer had told a public defender that she'd believed her stories would never lead to her arrest because she thought that police had solid evidence that Sufrich had been seen alive at a time when Sheirer had an alibi. She said she'd spun her stories from newspaper reports and a book about a California killing. The details of the murder, such as the exact position of the victim's body and head, she claimed, had been simply a matter of logic. The whole thing was a fabrication.

A psychiatrist hired by Sheirer's attorney, Brian Monahan, had initially diagnosed Sheirer with borderline personality disorder, with a history of substance abuse and depression. In a second interview, he confirmed it, but then he received a letter from her suggesting a diagnosis of multiple personality disorder. He undertook a third interview and decided this diagnosis was accurate. He would testify that she presented four alter personalities. "The Other Lori," who had penned the letter suggesting the diagnosis, had developed during the nine years when her father had sexually abused her (which he denied). "Annie" was a seductive personality who claimed to have enjoyed sex with her father and who worked as a prostitute. "Lori Ann" was an immature 12-year-old, and "Laura" was a nasty, angry, cocky personality.

Monahan also introduced mental health records with reports of blackouts and memory loss, a symptom common to cases of multiple personality. Other defense witnesses who were called to prove Sheirer's lack of credibility included a police chief and two detectives, to whom she had lied on several occasions. In addition, and more dramatically, under cross-examination, three of the five personalities revealed themselves.

Since the state lacked physical evidence connecting Sheirer to the murder scene and she was now recanting, they had a difficult case to prove. Apparently, the jury decided they had not done so, because after deliberating for eight hours, they acquitted Sheirer of all charges. This murder remains unsolved.

The Church Lady

This case is still pending, so we won't name the alleged perpetrator.

On January 23, 2008, Rhonda Smith, 42, of Hellertown, was found unconscious inside an office at Trinity Evangelical Lutheran Church on Route 212, bleeding from head wounds. She was transported to St. Luke's Hospital in the Valley, where she died. At first, there was talk of suicide, since Smith had suffered from a bipolar disorder, but she had been shot twice in the head and no gun was found at the scene. There appeared to be no reason why someone would kill Smith, who often volunteered at the church, yet her parents insisted she would not have killed herself.

Then late in March, a father and son out fishing found a .38 caliber handgun and some ammunition on the shore of Lake Nockamixon in Bucks County. It had been tossed recently, as there was no rust, and it was registered to a sixty-five-year-old woman who became an instant suspect. She, too, was a member of the church and was associated with an unsolved missing person case—that of her eighty-year-old father. An unstable, aggressive woman whom several people described as "threatening," she lived on a large piece of land that would now undergo a thorough search. Ballistics evidence confirmed that the gun was used in the shooting, so the woman was arrested. A story came out that she'd been jealous of the attention the church's pastor was paying to Smith, because she herself was infatuated with the man (and had stalked him). Apparently, she decided to eliminate the competition. She had called the church on the morning of January 23 to ask if Smith was coming in that day and received an affirmative response. After the murder occurred, she went to get her hair done and go shopping. As of this writing, a judge has ruled there's sufficient evidence to hold her for trial.

More Unsolved Mysteries

Northampton County Courthouse

In 1999, Northampton County District Attorney John Morganelli reviewed the area's 23 unsolved murders to take before a grand jury. He sent out letters to area police departments and made a list. Thanks to his attention to these crimes and new evidence or analysis, some were solved. Among the cases examined were:

- Cheryl van Horn, a single mother of three from Easton and rumored to be a police informant, was fatally shot in the chest on November 14, 1984, behind the Sheraton Inn at South 3rd Street and Larry Holmes Drive. Workers emptying trash found her fully clothed body. She had a drug problem and was an admitted prostitute, so her life circumstances made it difficult to identify a suspect.
- On September 12, 1997, at 7:00 A.M., the body of real estate agent Charlotte Fimiano, 40, was found in a vacant house on Chelsea Lane in Lower Saucon. She had been shot and strangled. Apparently she'd been showing a potential buyer the $259,000 home, but she'd left no information that would help with leads. The "cold call" appointment had been scheduled for 1:00 P.M. the day before, but Charlotte never returned to the office. Her husband reported her missing that evening, and the next day, her body was found. Similar deaths of realtors in other states provoked discussion of a mobile serial killer who knew how to lure lone female agents to secluded homes, although one was ever named.
- In 1982, a coroner's jury decided that Debra Deol's death was a homicide. The 27-year-old nurse was found dead in her bed on March 29, 1981,

covered by an electric blanket set on high (on an already warm day). The autopsy found 200 mg. of Lidocaine in her system, and a partially empty vial and syringe lay on a table next to the bed. She had died from respiratory arrest due to central nervous system hypersensitivity to the drug. Apparently she'd had sexual relations with someone the day before, although she was separated from her husband, Dr. Jasbir Deol, and had consumed food four hours before her death. Her mother, who insisted this was a homicide, pointed out that there were no food containers in the house. Yet no one was arrested.

- In 1993, Helen Weaver, 76, was strangled in her home on East Wilkes-Barre Street.
- Another elderly widow, Sarah Ziev, was suffocated after an unknown assailant broke into her home on Washington Street in 1960. He bound her to a bed, gagged her with a knotted bed sheet, and bludgeoned her with a blunt instrument. Detectives suspected robbery as a motive, since she'd supposedly kept a large sum of money in her home; they suspected that she and her killer were acquainted.
- Sandra Ann Miller, 22, was beaten and stabbed in her Nazareth home in 1978.
- David Allen Gross, 21, was found wrapped in a tarpaulin in the hatchback of his locked car on August 11, 1977, at an overlook in the Delaware Water Gap National Recreation Area.
- Julius Scheirer, 62, was struck in the head in his home in Lower Saucon Township in 1982.
- Several bodies found dumped in fields or along roadways include Walter Kupryczuk (1984), Kara Lee Lalaine (1987), and Robert Freeman, Sr. (1992).
- Ella C. Wunderly was beaten into unconsciousness during Christmas weekend in 1986 and her North Catasauqua home was ransacked. She died in a nursing home years later from pneumonia related to her injuries from the assault. Two teenagers were found guilty of the burglary, but not the assault. The grand jury recommended that one of them, Joseph Michael Strohl, who'd been Ella's neighbor at the time, be charged with second-degree murder. He went to trial, whereupon two eyewitnesses testified against him, and he was convicted. Later, his father indicated that Strohl had been home in bed on Christmas night, but could not account for his whereabouts for the entire weekend, so his testimony as an alibi witness was considered weak. Strohl continues to appeal.
- Eugene M. Zarate, 65, of Forks Township was a security guard at Palmer Storage Company, a self-storage facility in Palmer Township. Five days before Christmas in 1991, he was shot three times in the head. Fifty-one dollars remained in his billfold. While the responding officers initially believed it was a suicide, they finally realized that someone had killed

him. There was fingerprint, hair evidence and ballistic evidence from a .25 or .22 caliber handgun (although the killer took the bullet casings). The evidence went to the FBI lab for processing. The common theory is that he saw something he was not supposed to see, possibly evidence of criminal activity stored in one of the storage spaces, and had thus been eliminated.

- William Michael Sharkey, 49, was shot multiple times in October 1998, in Pocono Township and his body was then burned in his car. A hunter found the smoldering 1986 Chevrolet Caprice, *sans* license plate, in the early morning hours in the Delaware Water Gap National Recreation Area. It required an odontological analysis to identify the remains. He was last seen alive in his home around 7:30 on the evening prior.

- Twenty-two-year-old Kelly McBride, a young mother, went missing from her Northampton apartment in March 1984. Although her body was never found, her husband James gave her friends four different versions as to why she was gone: He said she'd left with another man, left with her father, gone to visit her mother, and gone to her lawyer to initiate divorce proceedings. Then upon his remarriage, McBride had lied on his marriage certificate when he claimed he'd never been married. He also lived in Florida under an assumed name and admittedly had used drugs in the 1980s. During the investigation, a witness turned up who claimed she'd seen Kelly fall and hit her head while the couple argued in their home. This same witness indicated she'd seen James put the body onto a bed and return with a handsaw; she also claimed to have seen him try to stuff the body into a dresser. A neighbor who saw McBride and his father remove a bloodstained mattress called the police, whereupon, she said, McBride had threatened her. Years later, mitochondrial DNA analysis of the mattress and a dresser from the home indicated the blood came from "a person conceived by Kelly McBride's parents." At trial, McBride took the stand in his own defense, but his version contradicted forensic reports and other witnesses. In 2001, the jury convicted him of first-degree murder and he received life in prison. He appealed, based on ineffective counsel, which the Pennsylvania Superior Court denied.

- Not on the list, because it was not in Northampton County, but also unsolved, is the 1995 murder in Salisbury Township of a 22-year-old Fountain Hill man, William A. Cornell. A man walking a dog on Constitution Avenue in the Upland Nature Preserve came across the badly decomposed remains. According to Lehigh County Coroner Scott Grim, Cornell had been bludgeoned repeatedly in the head. His body had been lying in the woods for some time, and he'd been missing for more than a month.

Also on Morganelli's list was Virginia Morrell, who was bound and gagged in her Easton apartment three decades ago, but this one was recently closed.

Halloween Murder

On Halloween night in 1978, someone entered Virginia Morrell's Anne Street apartment in Easton, raped and suffocated her by putting masking tape across her nose and mouth. Bound with her hands behind her back and left facedown and unclothed, the twenty-one-year-old also sustained cuts on her neck, chest, and leg. Clues at the scene were scant, except that a neighbor had overheard Virginia tell an unknown person to "leave me alone and get the hell out of here!" Police collected the ropes used to bind the victim and a nightgown from under her body. Two weeks later, Virginia's across-the-hall neighbor, a twenty-year-old man named Robert W. White, Jr., was accused of attempting to rape another woman. He was convicted and served his time, but since investigators found no evidence against him in the Morrell case, they could not press charges. Eventually he left town. Years went by and it appeared that the murder might go unsolved.

Easton Pennsylvania

However, during the 1990s, cold case squads formed nationwide to process older cases with new technologies, specifically DNA, unavailable in 1978. As part of this effort, Easton Police Detective Daniel Reagan began to look into the Morrell murder. It was the most brutal murder he'd seen in his three years as a detective. Since it had involved rape, he knew they had biological samples that could now be processed with scientific analysis. In April 2007, Reagan asked that this be performed on the nightgown found under Morrell's body. He also re-interviewed Robert White's former wife. (Cold case investigators count on changes in relationships over time to yield information once kept secret.) Barbara Williams-White said that she'd used a specific piece of rope for drying clothes in the bathroom, and on the night of the Morrell murder, she could not find it. It's not known whether detectives three decades ago showed her the rope used to bind

Virginia, but Reagan did. She said that one of the two ropes used looked like the one that had gone missing.

Reagan then went to interview White, who was now in Roanoke, Virginia, classified as a violent sex offender (thanks to the abduction and rape of a woman there). He denied knowing Morrell and said he'd never entered her apartment. However, the DNA analysis, processed through CODIS, where White's DNA was stored from other violent offenses, indicated that he was the perpetrator. This provided Reagan with probable cause to collect samples of White's DNA; the match was confirmed and White was arrested.

Thanks to good police work, the resolution of Virginia Morrell's brutal murder is one of the success stories. Hopefully, there will be more.

Gangster Hits

The 1920s saw several apparent organized hits in the Valley. On July 13, 1926, Louis Genovese was shot execution style in Allentown. He'd been invited to a card game at the Liberty Street home of Vinzenso Senape, which many believed was a set-up. A flurry of gunshots, heard by Senape's wife upstairs, left Genovese lying at the foot of the stairs in a pool of blood. The newspapers wrote about the "Vendetta," a supposed secret society of Italians and indicated that Genovese had been killed with nine bullets in the shape of a cross—supposedly this society's calling card. Apparently, there was some bad blood between Genovese and Senape over financial dealings, after Genovese refused to help Senape with a fine he owed. When police arrived on the scene, Senape claimed that robbers had entered the home, interrupting the card game, and shot Genovese, but since a single set of fresh footprints in the backyard matched Senape, the officers arrested him. However, he admitted to nothing. They were unable to make a case against him and he had a good lawyer, so he was released. No one else was ever arrested.

Two years later, another man died in a similar manner in Easton. The Black Horse Inn dated back to the 1700s, having once been a stagecoach stop and a way-station for people traveling on the Delaware River. It's now called Stemie's, located at 831 South Delaware Drive. In July 1928, Johnny Ferrara, aka, "Johnny the Wop," would often hang out there. One story has it that he kept money in the building, another that he was messing around with his boss's wife. In any event, he was on the phone in the hall when someone entered and unceremoniously whacked him. It was a hit, pure and simple, and as Johnny fell down the steps to the cellar, the perpetrator melted into the night. A beer delivery man found the body, and while an investigation ensued and a suspect was arrested and even brought to trial, no one was ever convicted of Johnny's murder.

This concludes our account. While we haven't covered all of the murders committed in the Valley, we've tried to offer those that were compelling for one reason or another. It's even possible that some of the unsolved cases might draw forth information that could assist cold case investigators. We hope so.

BIBLIOGRAPHY

Articles from the *Morning Call*, the *Pittsburgh Post-Gazette*, the *New York Times*, the *Philadelphia Inquirer*, the *Express-Times, Harrisburg Evening News* and the Harrisburg *Patriot*.

Adams, Lorraine. "Too Close for Comfort." *The Washington Post*, April 2, 1995.

Alexander, Max. "Killer on Call." *Reader's Digest*, November 2004.

"Angel of Death." A&E: Special Reports, February 2004.

Cullen, Charles. Interview transcript from the *Newark Star-Ledger*.

Durdock, Corrine. "Doctors ask that Howorth continue treatment." *East Penn Press*, July 1998.

Ellet, E. F. "The Fate of a Flirt of the Olden Time." *Godey's Lady's Book*, date unknown.

Hare, Robert. *Without Conscience: The Disturbing World of the Psychopaths among Us*. New York: Guilford, 1999.

Heindel, Ned D. *Hexenkopf: History, Healing and Hexerei*. Easton, PA: Williams Township Historical Society, 2005.

Kearney, John. *Lipstick and Blood*. Pinnacle Books, 2006.

Morganelli, John M. *The D-Day Bank Massacre: The True Story Behind the Martin Appel Case*. Pittsburgh, PA: Sterlinghouse, 2007.

Murder of the Geogles and the Lynching of the Fiend Snyder. Philadelphia: Barclay & Co., 1881.

Murder in the Family. A&E: Documentary, 1996.

Petherick, Wayne. *Serial Crime: Theoretical and Practical Issues in Behavioral Profiling*. Academic Press, 2005.

Ramsland, Katherine and Dana DeVito. *Bethlehem Ghosts*, Gettysburg, PA: Second Chance Publications, 2007.

Ramsland, Katherine. *Inside the Minds of Serial Killers*. Westport, CT: Praeger, 2006.

————*Inside the Minds of Healthcare Serial Killers*. Westport, CT: Praeger, 2007.

Reichel, Joe. Interview with Author and Zachary Lysek, 2008.

Rosen, Fred. *Blood Crimes: The Pennsylvania Skinhead Murders*. New York: Kensington, 1996.

————*Cosmopolitan*. March 1, 1996.

The Laros Tragedy. Easton, PA: West & Hilburn, 1876.

Woolley, Wayne. "Two Parricides linked at Trial." *York Daily Record*, October 10, 1995.

Zukowski, John. "Easton's Church Ghost Story: Tale Links beautiful Woman, Writer, and Place of Worship." *Express-Times*, October 31, 2003.

Katherine Ramsland teaches forensic psychology at DeSales University. She has published 33 books and over 600 articles. A former writer for Court TV's Crime Library, over the past decade, Ms. Ramsland has studied murder cases from around the world.

Other Books by Katherine Ramsland:

The Forensic Science of CSI
The CSI Effect
Beating the Devil's Game
The Human Predator
True Stories of CSI
The Devil's Dozen
Inside the Minds of Serial Killers
Inside the Minds of Mass Murders
Inside the Minds of Healthcare Serial Killers
The Science of Cold Case Files
Ghost: Investigating the Other Side
Cemetery Stories
The Heat Seekers
The Blood Hunters
The Science of Vampires
Piercing the Darkness: Undercover with Vampires in America Today
The Vampire Companion
The Witches' Companion
Bethlehem Ghosts